Carmel in th

A Pattern for Life
Rule of Saint Albert and the Carmelite Laity

Patrick Thomas McMahon, O.Carm.

A Pattern for Life
The Rule of Saint Albert and the Carmelite Laity

Edizioni Carmelitane

Copyright © 2007 by EDIZIONI CARMELITANE. All rights reserved. No part of this publication may be reproduced, stored in a retrieval system, or transmitted, in any form or by any means, electronic, mechanical, photocopying, recording, or otherwise, without the prior written permission of the publisher.

Cover: The photo on the cover is taken from a painting in the Carmelite hermitage in Christoval, Texas, modeled on the famous Lorenzetti Altarpiece originally made for the Carmelite Church in Siena.

ISBN 978-88-7288-095-1
ISSN 0394-7750

EDIZIONI CARMELITANE
Via Sforza Pallavicini, 10
00193 Roma / Italy
edizioni@ocarm.org

Since man's life on earth is a time of trial, and all who would live devotedly in Christ must undergo persecution, and the devil your foe is on the prowl like a roaring lion looking for prey to devour, you must use every care to clothe yourselves in God's armour so that you may be ready to withstand the enemy's ambush. Your loins are to be girt with chastity, your breast fortified by holy meditations, for, as Scripture has it, holy meditation will save you. Put on holiness as your breastplate, and it will enable you to love the Lord your God with all your heart and soul and strength, and your neighbour as yourself. Faith must be your shield on all occasions, and with it you will be able to quench all the flaming missiles of the wicked one: there can be no pleasing God without faith; [and the victory lies in this – your faith]. On your head set the helmet of salvation, and so be sure of deliverance by our only Saviour, who sets his own free from their sins. The Sword of the Spirit, the Word of God, must abound in your mouths and hearts. Let all you do have the Lord's Word for accompaniment.

To Rose Wilhelm of the Lay Carmelite Office, Darien, who is far more than a secretary and to whom the Lay Carmelites in the United States owe far more than they will ever realize.

INDEX

Preface 9

Introduction 11

The Background 15

The Text and Commentary 83

Some Closing Considerations 217

A Final Reflection 229

PREFACE

This year we celebrate the eighth centenary of the Carmelite Rule. We do not know the exact date when the Patriarch of Jerusalem, Albert of Vercelli, delivered to a small group of hermits living on Mount Carmel a simple document outlining for them at their request, a pattern for living a holy life, a life of discipleship of Jesus Christ. We do know that it had to be between his arrival in the Holy Land in 1206 and his death in 1214. There is actually much we do not know about these hermits, but the letter he wrote them outlining how he thought they should live gives us a window into their experience of striving to be faithful to Christ. These hermits were not monks. There may have been a priest or two in the group, but they were mostly laymen interested in a devout life of submission to Jesus Christ and to his Gospel. They were one of many groups of lay hermits in the twelfth and thirteenth centuries. Albert probably had no idea that eight centuries later men and women would still be following the pattern of life that he laid out for these hermits. He certainly could not have envisioned the complexities of our modern world and how his simple document would be adjusted to fit Friars and cloistered Nuns and nursing Sisters, and Lay People too, in the far flung corners of the globe and in lands of which he had never heard. Yet for eight centuries this simple letter he wrote the hermits on Mount Carmel has provided a spiritual vision for some of the greatest saints of the Church and it continues today for many saints-in-the-making.

There has been much debate in the last ten years or so about the Rule of Saint Albert and its suitability for the laity. Some think that the Carmelite Laity need a separate Rule, that the Rule of Saint Albert is suited only to the Religious Life. Others see that it is the Rule of Saint Albert, or rather following the Rule of Saint Albert, that makes one a Carmelite and that it is eminently suitable for any and for all in the Carmelite family.

I hope in this short book to look at the Rule of Saint Albert, or perhaps better to call it by its original title, the *Pattern for Life* which Albert gave the hermits, and open it up to the reflection of a Lay Carmelite audience so that they can see for themselves that the text speaks to all who would lead a live of allegiance to Jesus Christ in Carmel. It is my hope that you will find continuous inspiration in this letter of a Bishop to some hermits to guide you on your spiritual journey as well.

INTRODUCTION

In July 2005 a group of Carmelite scholars met in Lisieux France to study the Rule of Saint Albert in preparation for the eighth centenary of the foundation of the Carmelite Order when Albert of Jerusalem, the Latin Patriarch, issued a simple *Formula Vitae* or Pattern for Life for a small community of lay hermits that were living in the wadi 'ain es-Siah, a river bed on the southern slopes of Mount Carmel facing the Mediterranean Sea, just south of the modern city of Haifa.

Very little is known about the early Carmelites. Their foundation in the Crusader Kingdom at the end of the Third Crusade and the subsequent political instability of the region which caused the original community on Mount Carmel to flee less than a century after the foundation has left us with almost no historical records of the early years of the Order. Unlike the other Religious Orders founded at that time, the Franciscans and Dominicans for example, we do not even know the names of the founder or founders of the community. One of the few artefacts we do have from the period, and we have this only in a later copy and edition, is the Rule which the Patriarch gave them to follow as a way of life. That way of life would be modified in 1247 by Pope Innocent IV and it is the modified Rule that we Carmelites follow today.

The seminar in Lisieux was amazing for the insights that study provided into this central document of our Carmelite heritage. Several years previously, the Discalced Carmelites had held a seminar on Mount Carmel and provided a series of studies of how the Rule is understood today in various different cultures in which Carmel finds itself. These papers were published both on the Internet and in book form as *Rule of Carmel: New Horizons* and provide much stimulating thought and discussion on how we might live this document today. We did not want to reduplicate the efforts of our Discalced brothers and sisters, however, and so we approached the Rule from several different standpoints. We did look at how it might be understood from different cultural perspectives, but we concentrated on looking at historical and textual studies that explored the Rule in its historical context and from the perspective of how the text was constructed and what the text actually says. It was a fascinating experience. One of the most valuable studies was that of Father Craig Morrison, O.Carm. of the Pontifical Biblical Institute. Father Craig did a detailed analysis of how Albert used scripture in the Rule. In the process he revealed much about Albert's spiritual depths and the spirituality he was nurturing in the hermits under his care. Brother Patrick Mullins, O.Carm., Dean of Theology at the Milltown Institute in Dublin and president of the Carmelite Institute of Britain and Ireland, also wrote an invaluable paper. Doctor Mullins made a very crucial connection between Albert's calling the hermits to live *in obsequio Ihesu Christi*–allegiance to Jesus Christ–and the chapters on spiritual warfare (numbers 18 and 19) in the Rule. This connection will provide a central theme for this current book. There were other extraordinary papers as well.

This book is intended for Lay Carmelites and not for the scholarly community and it does not attempt to synthesize the work of that congress. The papers given at that Congress will be published in a more erudite format worthy of them. My interest in this book is reaching the Lay Carmelite audience with material that is substantive but aimed at a practical understanding of the Rule of Saint Albert. The scholarship presented at the Lisieux seminar is far more detailed that we need for the scope of this book, but this book does draw on that work to offer the reader insights of how the Rule might be best applied to Lay Carmelites in the ninth century of our Carmelite life. The best use that might be made for a book like this is to provide discussion for Lay Carmelite communities to explore together the meaning of the Rule for themselves in the concrete situations in which they live. In other words, the reflections and discussion of the readers is as important as anything I present.

The book is written in three sections. The first provides a historical overlook at the background of the Rule. A little knowledge about the evolution of monastic spirituality, Lay hermits, the Crusades, the spirituality of the thirteenth century, and other religious movements of the time will help the reader appreciate the Rule in its context. The second section provides a chapter by chapter look at the *Pattern for Life* that Albert gave the hermits. The changes made by the commissioners of Pope Innocent IV in 1247 are clearly noted, and text is discussed in both its historical sense and with some ideas of what it might offer a modern Lay Carmelite reader. Finally, the third section draws some broad summaries and conclusions that Lay Carmelites may want to think about and discuss as they explore living our Carmelite vocation in their state of life.

Several issues are raised in the study more than once. The Rule, for example, treats the virtue of chastity in two places and I have discussed it in both sections without trying to make the conversation redundant. The topic of *in obsequio Ihesu Christi*, allegiance to Jesus Christ, so central to the Rule, and its relationship to the chapter on Spiritual Warfare also comes up more than once, indeed it often seems to be a thread running through the entire discussion, but that is because I have come to believe that it is the fundamental concept in the Rule. The lay status of the hermits is discussed in several different places, as is the difference between a Rule and a *Formula Vitae* or Pattern for Life. These again are elemental topics that merit considerable attention if we are to understand how this document might apply not only to the Religious but to the Laity of the Order.

All in all, I hope that this book benefits our Lay Carmelites and shows you that Albert's *Pattern for Life*, much in the spirit of Vatican II's theology of the Universal Call to Holiness, fits us all, Religious and Laity, in the Carmelite family and will help the reader live his or her Carmelite vocation ever more deeply and abundantly in grace.

The Background
The Monks of Long Ago

How strange it must have been to be the first monk. There was no monastery to go to. There was no novice master to teach the way. There was no habit to wear. There was no Rule to follow. Indeed, at the beginning, there were only ordinary Christians, lay people, who wanted something more out of their faith than was being asked of them in the Church. Contemporary scholarship indicates that these first people to follow what we now recognize as a monastic vocation emerged in the Church of Syria in the second century.[1] It began simply enough. Adults, often converts at the time of their baptism, might make a vow to remain unmarried in imitation of Christ. They would live a single life as a visible reminder to the Christian Community of Christ who was the "single-one (the only-begotten) of the Father."

These "single-ones" were lay people. They did not wear a habit. They did not go off to monasteries. They stayed in their family homes where they gave themselves to prayer. They became family-servants, doing

---

[1] For more information on this, see Sydney Griffith, "Asceticism in the Church of Syria: The Hermeneutics of Early Syrian Monasticism," *Asceticism*, ed. Vincent L. Wimbush and Richard Valantasis, New York: Oxford University Press, 1995.

the domestic work of the family in return for their support. For the women, bound as they were to the restricted social roles of women in the Roman world and Syrian culture, this was not a drastic change, but for the men it was revolutionary. Men were expected to take part in public life as citizens, but these consecrated men remained home, not only doing servants' work but renouncing the privileges of citizenship in exchange for dedicating their lives to Christ. Work and prayer was the vocation of these men and women. They did not go out for social events, many apparently did not even go out to church for worship. Hidden within the family, inconspicuous in every way, they worked through the day at simple tasks and through the hours of the night they prayed the scriptures, mediating on the Word of the Lord.

The custom also arose in the early Church of the East–Syria, Palestine, Egypt–of women putting themselves under the protection of the Church rather than marrying. These women might be unmarried young women or widows who wished not to remarry. It was very difficult for women of that time and place to remain unmarried. In the world of the Roman Empire and under Roman Law, a woman had no standing of her own before the law and thus required the legal protection of a man. A woman was under the authority of her father until he "gave her away" to her husband. When widowed, the oldest son was responsible for her. One way for a woman to escape this system of family control was to put herself under the protection and responsibility of the Church. Such women lived secluded lives in a house with other women consecrated to celibacy and who gave themselves over to the work of the church–sewing clothes for the poor, feeding the poor and sick, preparing the Eucharistic bread for the Liturgy, and other tasks, combined, of course, with prayer.

In the third century there were men and women (though far more men than women given the physical dangers and hardship of the life, as well as the difficulty women faced in escaping family control) who went off into the deserts of Egypt or Syria as hermits. Many of these were discouraged with the world in which they lived. They found the world too materialistic, too violent, too political. They often were disenchanted with the Church as well, finding it not demanding enough, not challenging enough, too conformed to the ways of Roman society. They remembered the martyrs who gave their lives in testimony to their faith and they wanted a faith that challenged them to look deeply into themselves and see the spiritual battle that had to be fought if their hearts were to be surrendered to Christ. In the solitude of the desert they could give themselves over to fasts, to ascetical practice, to prayer, to self-examination. Some of these hermits were quite eccentric–living totally naked, or standing for days on one foot, or chasing away people coming to seek advice and guidance. Some of them were undoubtedly insane. It is not healthy for people to live as total solitaries. From the beginning God knew that humans need company of other humans. But the wiser and saner of these hermits inspired others to seek God in solitude. In Egypt, towards the beginning of the fourth century, one of these early desert fathers, Pachomius, began organizing his hermit-disciples into communities for mutual support and guidance. Monasteries began. Up until this point, however, the monastic life was totally in the context of a lay life. Monks and nuns were ordinary people living extraordinarily prayerful lives hidden away in the corners of the world, practically invisible except to the eye of those who were sensitive to the spiritual life.

For centuries monasticism would remain a lay movement. Monasticism only slowly became a distinct vocation in the Church. Originally monks and nuns were forbidden to dress differently than other Christians. Those in the desert tended to wear ordinary peasant dress suitable for the agricultural work that supported them, usually just a sleeveless shift of unbleached linen that reached to the knees with a shawl of the same material to cover their head against the sun or wrap around their shoulders in the evening air. By the fourth century they began in many places, especially in the towns and cities of Asia Minor, to adopt a large-sleeved gown of black cloth over their work clothes when they were not in the fields. For both monks and nuns, veiling their heads was a sign of their consecration to chastity. In the west, the veil eventually became a hood for the men. Until the twelfth century most monks were not ordained priests. Other changes evolved as well. Sadly, in the western Church, the monastic life became more and more limited to the children of land-owning families, that is, to the nobility and the knightly class. There was no place for the sons and daughters of the peasants to find a religious vocation. That began to change in the eleventh and twelfth centuries. The Cistercian monks began taking peasants, not as full monks but as Lay Brothers, to do the heavy agricultural work to which they were by birth accustomed.

With the revival of European economy in the eleventh and twelfth centuries, an urban middle class emerged. There would need to be a place for the young men and women of these families to find a way to live a more deep spiritual life.

The hermits

Hermits were a frequent occurrence in the Middle Ages–far more common than they are in our world today–but they were anything but uniform. Some hermits were monks–members of the Benedictine or Cistercian orders who had permission from their abbot to live, not in the monastery, but in a cell apart, even miles away, from their monastery. Permission to live as a hermit was only granted to the most mature of monks as the hermit life was understood to be only for the spiritually advanced, those who had polished their spiritual journey by years of communal living. Others belonged to monastic orders of hermits–orders like the Carthusians or the Camaldolese Benedictines–in which all the choir monks were expected to live in hermitages and gather together only for the Divine Office and an occasional community meal. There were also lay hermits–indeed probably more lay hermits than monastic ones. These were men, almost invariably men, from a variety of social classes from the wealthy to the peasant, who eschewed traditional religious life, but wanted a simple life of solitude and labour in which they could follow some inner call to deep communion with God.

Lay hermits differed tremendously among themselves. They were not monks, indeed they were not Religious. Some lived in hermit colonies with a leader. Others lived as solitaries. Some manned lighthouses or lived by a bridge and kept it in repair in return for material support. Most did some sort of manual labour to support themselves. Some accepted alms in return for prayers. Many wandered the countryside or into the towns, speaking of Christ and the Gospels to whomever would listen. They often were especially kind to lepers and other social outcasts, sharing their food with them and accepting the company of those whom society rejected.

While anyone might contrive to find a way to live by himself and devote himself to prayer and work, one could not just go off and decide to become a hermit. If a monk wished to become a hermit, permission of his abbot and community were required. Lay hermits needed the permission and blessing of the bishop. This blessing gave the hermit a quasi-canonical status. It did not make him a cleric or a Religious, but it did put him under the protection of the Church as regards the civil law. If he was accused of a crime he would be tried by the bishop's court, not the civil courts and he was protected from capital punishment. It also gave him the right to wear the distinctive dress of hermits and to accept alms for his support. Hermits typically wore a tunic gathered with a leather belt. The tunic was not full length as for the clergy and Religious, but was mid-calf, far longer than was fashionable in the twelfth and thirteenth centuries. They also wore a short cape with a hood. Canonical pilgrims–that is pilgrims who had sought and received the blessing of the bishop on their pilgrimage–wore the same habit and had the same right to receive alms while on their journey. Pilgrims moreover could wear a purse on their belt in which they carried their papers and whatever food had been given them in the way of alms. Neither hermits nor pilgrims usually received money as alms, but kind people often gave them food in return for prayers. They were to go on their journeys poor as Christ sent his apostles, with no coin, nor second shirt, nor sandals, nor walking stick. Often hermits became pilgrims and set out for various holy places–the tombs of the Apostles in Rome, the shrine of Saint James at Compostella, Thomas Becket's tomb at Canterbury, and especially the Holy Land. When pilgrims and hermits went to the Holy Land they often remained there, pilgrims settling down as hermits in the land where Christ had walked. They wanted to see with their eyes what he had seen with his, and to follow in his footsteps as a way of better knowing and serving him.

The Holy Land

Christian pilgrims had come to the Holy Land for centuries, certainly since the time of Constantine the Great in the fourth century and even before to visit the sites where Christ had been born, lived, died, and was raised. And there had long been monks and nuns in the Holy Land–indeed the Holy Land was part of the cradle of the monastic life as far back as the fourth century. But in 638 the Arabs had conquered the Land of Christ and the new rulers of the land were Muslim. Now, Jesus figures prominently in the Qu'ran and is venerated as one of the great prophets by Muslims. Furthermore, his mother Mary is venerated as well. Mohammed had told his disciples not to force Jews or Christians to join the new religion and the Muslim overlords of the Land were, in general, quite tolerant of the Christians living there. Christian pilgrims continued to come and go to the Holy Places and while most of the monasteries in the Holy Land followed either the Greek or Syrian Orthodox faith, pilgrims from the Catholic west found welcome as well–at least if they were willing to pay the various tolls and taxes to the Muslim overlords.

Two things happened in the eleventh century to change the course of events in the Holy Land and pave the way for our Latin hermits to come and settle on Mount Carmel. The first was that in 1009 the "Mad Caliph," Al-Hakim, turned on the Christians and ordered the destruction of the Holy Sepulchre. This act of desecration outraged Christians around the world. The second event was in 1054 the Pope of Rome and the Patriarch of Constantinople excommunicated each other and in doing so shattered the unity of the Church.

At the end of the eleventh century, Pope Urban II saw a way that he hoped would restore the unity of Christians. The Arab empire was brushing up against and slowly devouring the Byzantine Empire of Constantinople. The Pope called on Catholic Christians to mount a war of conquest to take back the Holy Land for Christians. This would protect the holy places from any future desecration, and give western pilgrims easier access to the shrines. Even more important to the Pope, however, it would defend the Byzantine Empire. The Pope was hopeful that a grateful emperor would compel the Greek Church to reunite with Rome. In the event, the crusade was a military success. The Land was won for Christianity. But the hoped for reunion was not to happen. In fact, when Crusaders attacked and sacked the city of Constantinople in 1204, it generated a bitter resentment on the part of the Greeks that keeps the Churches divided to this day. But that is not part of our story.

On July 15, 1099 Jerusalem fell to the Crusaders. The Land was once again under Christian rule, but the rule of a Christian minority. The Christians in the Holy Land were not Catholic but mostly Greek, Syrian, and Armenian Christians. The Crusaders permitted the various Eastern Christians to keep their traditional rites, but forced them to submit to Latin (Catholic) authority. The Greek Patriarch was replaced by a Latin Catholic Patriarch and the various schismatic bishops forced to unite with Rome under the authority of the Latin Patriarch. The Greeks and Syrians and Armenians were not happy about this, but had little choice. The Crusaders divided up the Holy Land into various principalities and duchies under leading crusader lords. Baldwin, a Frenchman, was

King of Jerusalem. Pilgrims flocked to the Holy Land to visit the places where Christ had lived. Merchants flocked to the Holy Land to buy the precious goods–silks and fabrics, porcelains, spices and herbs, Arab horses, and all sorts of exotic goods–that they could bring back to the markets of Europe. Adventurers came to make their fortunes. The poor scratched together enough money for passage hoping to find work and opportunity in the newly opened lands. And hermits came to pray and imitate Christ's apostles. But it was not to last.

The native people had a deep resentment about these Latins. The Greeks and Syrians and Armenians did not like being forced into Catholicism. The Arabs were unhappy that their leaders had been driven from the land. Muslims resented the taxes and harassment they suffered at the hands of the Crusaders. The land roiled in trouble. And then, towards the end of the twelfth century, a brilliant Arab General, Saladin, appeared and with a lightening speed all but drove the Crusaders out. Jerusalem fell to the Arabs, then castle after castle, town after town, until the Crusaders and the Latins were penned up in the coastal city of Tyre waiting for ships to come to evacuate them back to Europe.

The ships came, but with the ships came three great kings–Richard the Lionhearted, Philip Augustus of France, and the Emperor Frederick. The Crusades were on again and this, the Third Crusade, pushed Saladin back–not all the way to Jerusalem, he kept that–but far enough back to carve out a new Crusader kingdom with its capital at Acre, just north of Haifa.

The Latins–merchants, adventurers, hangers-on, ne'er-do-wells, and yes, hermits, swarmed out of Tyre and repopulated the land. It was then that hermits, probably one by one, began settling on the south-western slope of Mount Carmel at a place called the wadi, or creek, 'ain es-Siah.

We know no details of these hermits. We have no names with any surety. We don't know their various lands of origin. Were there any priests among them? We don't know. Certainly one or two of them may have been priests. One or two may even have been monk-hermits who had become detached from their abbeys by pilgrimage. But in general they were neither Clergy nor Religious. Nor were they Crusaders themselves. Members of the knightly class did not become lay hermits. They might enter religion in the Orders of Knights-monastic such as the Templars or the Knights of the Hospital of Saint John of Jerusalem–both of which were approved Religious orders whose members followed a Rule and professed Solemn Vows of Poverty, Chastity, and Obedience. Most probably had been hermits somewhere before–in Europe or in the Holy Land. Most had probably come to the Holy Land as pilgrims. Some perhaps had come in other capacities and once in the Land of Christ felt called to follow Christ as a hermit. At the end of the day however we simply know very little for sure about them. No records survive.

What we do know is that at some point they banded together and chose a leader. We do not know his name, but the bishop will refer to him as Brother B. Tradition says his name was Brocard and it may well have been. And then, to properly constitute themselves as lay hermits, they went to seek approval from the Latin Patriarch of Jerusalem who lived in nearby Acre–Jerusalem itself being still in Muslim hands.

The Bishop

Albert was born to the noble family of the Counts of Avogardo at Castle Gualtieri, not far from Parma in Italy in or around 1149. He studied law and theology before entering the Order of the Canons Regular of the Holy Cross at Mortara where he was elected prior at the age of 30. Four years later he was named Bishop of Bobbio and then translated to the arch-episcopal see of Vercelli the following year. He was selected by both the Emperor Frederick Barbarosa and Pope Clement III to mediate their disputes and achieved peace between the papal and imperial factions in 1189. He was named papal legate to mediate an end to the war between Parma and Piacenza in 1199 and then in 1205 was named to the prestigious post of Patriarch of Jerusalem.

Albert arrived in the Holy Land in 1206 but never was able to take possession of his see which was held by the Muslim forces under the Ayyubid Kurd general Saladin. He established himself in the crusader capital of Acre only a few miles distant from Mount Carmel. Acre was itself a diocese with its own bishop, but Albert's authority superseded the local bishop since Albert was not only bishop of Jerusalem, but Patriarch over the entire Holy Land *and* a Papal Legate.[2] Albert was obviously a busy man with many responsibilities. Indeed, he was one of the most powerful prelates in the Church holding title to the most ancient of sees and serving as the pope's lieutenant in the Crusader world. In an age before modern communications, papal legates had the authority–and used the authority–to make decisions normally referred to the papal court. This required the legate to be a man who knew the canon law well and could "second-guess" the pope on important decisions. It also meant, of course, that any person appointed to this position, had the full confidence of the pope.

After a career of peacemaking, Albert died ironically as a victim of violence. He had angered a clergyman by firing him from his post as a hospital-administrator and the cleric attacked the patriarch with a knife, murdering him during the procession for the Feast of the Holy Cross, September 14th, 1214 at Acre. Albert had planned on returning to Europe to attend the fourth Lateran Council held in 1215. Had he lived and attended this council he may well have gone on to succeeded Pope Innocent III at his death in 1216. That, of course, did not happen. He was regarded, however, as one of the most competent churchmen of his time, both as a diplomat and as a canon lawyer.

While Archbishop of Vercelli, Albert had been asked by Pope Innocent III to chair a commission to

---

[2] The Latin hermits, by the way, were not in the diocese of Acre despite their closeness to the capital, but in the diocese of Caesarea. Cicconetti, *The Rule of Carmel*, pp. 70-71.

prepare a Rule for a new Religious order that was being established called the Umiliati. The Umiliati were originally members of a spontaneous religious movement that arose among workers in the cloth industry of Lombardy who wished to become a canonical Religious order. It was Albert and the commission that he chaired that created the division, for the first time, of first, second, and third orders as a way to create communities for both celibate men and celibate women as well as affiliating married laity to those communities.

In the Holy Land Albert had a large chancery of canon lawyers and various specialists to assist him in his work. His life was a busy one, and his responsibilities were considerable. In addition to the affairs of his own patriarchal see, and the See of Acre which he looked after while it was empty, he had oversight of all the dioceses of the Holy Land, including those of the Greeks, Syrians, and Armenians who had been forcibly subordinated to the authority of the Pope and his legate in the Holy Land. In these matters he had to be sensitive to the differing canon law, rites, and traditions of each distinct group. Albert was faced with many problems in his jurisdiction, not least of which was the failure of the crusades. Jerusalem was again in Muslim hands and there was no immediate prospect of winning it back. The kings had come and the kings had returned to their kingdoms in France and England and Germany with Jerusalem uncaptured. The Crusader position in the land was at best tenuous. There were too few knights to defend the land and too often those knights were busy fighting among themselves. Most Christians resented Albert's authority–and the authority of the Latin's in general–over them. The Syrians, Greeks, and Armenians made it clear that they would be happier under the very just rule of the competent Saladin who had reinstalled a Greek Patriarch at the Church of the Holy Sepulchre and freed the Christians under him of Latin domination. How could the papal legate hold the land for Christ and his Church?

It was to this man, both competent and busy, that the hermits came asking for him to grant them his ecclesiastical approval. They seem to have proposed to him their ideas about how they should live as he makes mention of "your proposal" in his letter back to them. But he did not simply dismiss them with a routine approval of their proposal. He seems to have taken their proposal and reworked it, adding considerable insights of his own, and even–I believe–redefining their mission in a way that made them central to the whole purpose of the crusades. But first, let's look at their proposal.

A Way of Life

We do not know what the proposal that the hermits made to Albert looked like. There is no text available. Indeed, there may never have been an actual text. The hermits, or their leaders, may simply have met with Albert and discussed briefly what they believed was essential to their life. But we cannot ignore that he does mention a certain *propositum vestrum*, "your proposal." Perhaps it was no more than a request. Perhaps they offered him no suggestions about the way of life he was to define for them. But that is unlikely. Some, if not most, of these men were seasoned hermits. They had already been together long enough to choose a leader. They had to have some idea of what their life should be like.

Several years ago there was a conference in Lisieux in France of Carmelites to study the Rule. Many excellent papers were given at that conference. One of the most interesting was a paper by the Carmelite Biblicist, Father Craig Morrison who teaches at the Pontifical Biblical Institute in Rome. Father Craig did a very careful analysis of how Albert used scripture in the Rule he wrote for the hermits. When we see how Albert used scripture to explain to the hermits his ideas regarding how they should live, we get a clear sense of Albert's vision for the hermits. We also get a sense of his particular style of moulding the Scriptural texts around the ideas he wants to impress on the hermits. Perhaps if we subtract the passages that demonstrate Albert's use of scripture to express his opinions, we can see the parts of the text that may not be from Albert, that is, the parts of the Rule that incorporate the proposal of the hermits. Admittedly this is not a terribly scientific approach, and we don't want to take this as anything more than a conjecture, but when one sees how Albert used scripture–constantly and consistently used scripture–those passages which are bereft of scriptural texts look curious and strange. They seem oddly different in tone. I would like to suggest that the following may be a re-creation of the hermit's proposal for their way of life.

We are to have a prior, one of ourselves, who is to be chosen for the office by common consent, or that of the greater and more mature part, each of the others must promise him obedience

Next, each one of us is to have a separate cell, situated as the lie of the land may dictate, and allotted by disposition of the prior with the agreement of the other brothers, or the more mature among them. None of the brothers is to occupy a cell other than that allotted to him or to exchange cells with another, without leave or whoever is prior at the time.

The prior's cell should stand near the entrance to the place, so that he may be the first to meet those who approach, and determine what business must be done. Each one is to stay in his own cell or nearby unless attending to some other duty. We are to give ourselves to work of some kind for our support. Our day, and even more the night, should be governed by silence.

Those who know their letters and how to read the psalms, should, for each of the hours, say those our holy predecessors laid down and the approved custom of the Church appoints for that hour Those who do not know their letters must say twenty-five 'Our Fathers" for the night Office, except on Sundays and solemnities when the number is to be doubled so that the 'Our Father' is said fifty times; the same prayer must be said seven times in the morning in place of Lauds and seven times too for each of the other hours, except for Vespers when it must be said fifteen times.

None must lay claim to anything as his own, but all goods are to be held in common. However, each one is to stay in his allotted cell, and live by himself on what is given out to him.

An oratory should be built among the cells, where, if it can be done without difficulty, we are to gather each morning to solemnly hear Mass. On Sundays too, or other days if necessary, we should discuss matters of discipline and our spiritual welfare; and on this occasion the indiscretions and failings of the members of the community, if any be found at fault, should be corrected with due charity.

We are to fast every day, except Sundays, from the feast of the Exaltation of the Holy Cross until Easter Day, unless bodily sickness or feebleness, or some other good reason demand a dispensation from the fast. We are always to abstain from meat, unless it has to be eaten as a remedy for sickness or great feebleness.

Is it fair to rule out any scriptural reference as being from the hermit's proposal? No, of course not. The hermits may well have peppered their proposal with scripture. But Craig Morrison's study indicates the very artful way that scripture is used in the Rule was the work of a single author, a very sophisticated author who knew monastic spirituality very deeply, and who knew how to wrap the scriptures around both the spiritual depths and the practical necessities of life. That is what makes those passages that do not reference the scriptures appear so strangely different. Of course there may be parts of their original proposal that we cannot find, parts that lie beneath chapters that Albert totally rewrote using his methodology of quoting, paraphrasing, alluding to, and mix-and-matching scripture. There also may have even been parts where Albert removed a scriptural reference from the hermit's proposal, though it would be unclear why he might do this. We also should look at the remaining text, the text that I am attributing to the hermits, and see if there are traces of Cassian or other authors that would more likely–though not necessarily–be from Albert's pen. As I said, this is not a very scientific reconstruction. We really cannot say what the "*propositum vestrum*" looked like with any certitude. But the above text would spell out the essentials that Albert used as the foundation and building blocks for the way of life he envisioned for the hermits. It is curious to note that almost all of the above text lies in the first half of the Way of Life that Albert would eventually give the hermits. It would seem that Albert may have taken the proposal, embroidered it with several small bits and pieces of scripture, and then added on a vision of his own–much richer and deeper than the fairly simple norms in the first half of the text. If this breakdown is at all accurate it would indicate that the hermits had a simple vision of their project and Albert had much greater hopes for them.

How the hermits understood their vocation

While the text in the previous section may not be a completely reliable reconstruction of the hermits original proposal it is Albert's *Way of Life* minus what is clearly Albert's contribution and it can give us at least a rough idea of how the hermits viewed their vocation when they went to Albert seeking his approval. It was pretty minimalist. It is not unlikely that there were passages that Albert rewrote in his richly scriptural style leaving no trace of the hermits original wording but keeping the actual *propositum*. An example of this might be the passages on work and on silence. There were possibly passages he removed all together. But even in what is left there is the outline of a simple eremitical life. It is a loosely knit settlement of hermits, coordinated by a senior brother chosen by and from among the brothers, who have pretty minimal contact with one another. They gather daily for Mass–when possible–and weekly for a discussion of their common life and mutual correction and encouragement. Other than that they stay in their cells or adjoining gardens, giving themselves over the recitation of the psalms or other prayers according to their abilities, and working.

Why such a minimalist approach? Joachim Smet and several others suggest–and quite reasonably–that these hermits gathered from very different backgrounds. Many had probably been part of hermit communities in other places both in the Holy Land and probably in Europe. When with the military advance of Saladin the Latins had been forced to flee from their homes throughout the Crusader kingdom and find refuge in Tyre, many hermit communities undoubtedly disbanded. After the re-conquest of the Galilee, hermits who had formerly lived in Jerusalem or Judea or the Jordan valley probably did not feel safe living in Muslim lands. (Some did return–Bishop Jacques de Vitry, a decade after Albert's death, leaves testimony to hermits settled in the desert near the Jordan where Christ endured the forty days of fasting and temptation.) The settlement on Mount Carmel then would represent hermits coming from different places with different traditions. A loosely-formed *Way of Life* would allow maximum room for each to live out his spiritual life in the ways with which he was familiar. Old dogs don't take to new tricks and old hermits get quite settled in their ways. A minimum of structure permitted each the room he needed to live out his vocation. Yet there are some surprising elements that are in the proposal and some that are surprising for not being there.

The most notable absence is there is no provision for a common meal, at least weekly or on occasion. That is not to say that the hermits may not have gathered for a meal from time to time, but even the strictest hermit monks, the Carthusians, had a weekly meal in common. The common table was a sign of the evangelical life, an imitation of Christ and the apostles who regularly ate together. Common meals had a sacred significance, a significance that modern western society has for the most part lost. Orthodox Jews eat with their heads covered because the common table, even with its wine and its laughter and song–and sometimes dance–are seen to be a prayer. Monastic communities too have highly ritualized mealtimes because the meal together is seen to be part of the prayer life of the community. Practically all the other religious groups of the twelfth and thirteenth century made the common table an essential part of their life, but not the hermits on Mount Carmel. Fast and abstinence are prescribed, but the *Way of Life* that Albert would provide for them, and most probably their original proposal, make no provision for eating together on any occasion. It is very strange. It does, however, give the individual hermit some discretionary judgement over when he would have his meals, and even–given the bounds of the fast–how he would portion out the food allotted him. It also would allow for variations in diet–again given the limitations of the fast and the dependency of the hermit on the community for food–that at the common table might draw attention to the individual. For example, if one hermit decided that his fasting would include not eating any dairy products, a common form of fast especially in the Near East, his rigor would attract attention at a common table where dairy was not prohibited to all. Eating singly allowed the hermit more discretionary control over the rigors of his diet. Nonetheless, it is strange given the emphasis on common table among Religious of the time.

A surprising norm that is found in the Way of Life, and again would seem to be part of the hermit's proposal, is the requirement for daily Mass–when possible. While daily Mass was common in Religious communities by the thirteenth century, it is not found in most Rules. Benedict's Rule was written at a time when daily Eucharist would be found only in cathedral churches, and often not even there. Daily Mass came slowly into the monasteries of Europe, probably only becoming normal at the time of the Carolingian reforms of the late eighth century. Augustine's Rule, the most commonly used Rule of the Middle Ages, was unfamiliar with the practice, though again by the tenth and eleventh centuries the canons regular would have normally had a daily conventual Mass. Francis did not prescribe daily Mass in his Rule, but certainly by the thirteenth century it was normative in any community where there was at least one priest to celebrate.

What makes the requirement of daily Mass particularly strange in the *Way of Life* is that the hermits could not have had Mass at all until Albert approved their proposal. He had to grant them permission to build an oratory and until that oratory was built and its altar consecrated, the hermits could not have had Mass in their settlement. In the Middle Ages Christians were not at all cavalier about having Mass at any old place and on any old table they could find. The canon law was very strict on this and while the practice of a "portable altar"—a altar stone that could be carried in a saddle bag by a prelate and used while travelling—was spreading about this very time, the circumstances under which Mass could be celebrated were highly regulated. The hermits had to have been in the practice of hiking from their valley retreat to the nearest church which Elias Friedman claims was perhaps two kilometres distant.[3] The proposal for constructing an oratory and holding a daily Mass indicates that there very like-

---

[3] Elias Friedman, *The Latin Hermits of Mount Carmel*, Rome, 1979. The fortified village of Castle-Anne probably would have been the site of the nearest church.

ly was at least one priest among the hermits. We cannot be sure of that of course, but their confidence that daily Mass was a normal possibility would give us some indication that a priest was available from within the hermit community.

In mentioning the daily Mass we should also pay attention to the fact that while they were hearing Mass each day, they were not normally receiving communion. Daily communion was unheard of in the Middle Ages. Priests would receive whenever they celebrated, of course, but for those not in the priesthood, the reception of Holy Communion might only be a few times a year. Indeed in 1215, at the Fourth Ecumenical Council of the Lateran, the Church had to make it a law that Catholics had to receive Holy Communion at least annually and that during the period of Lent/Eastertide. The fact that such a law was required tells us that many were not even receiving annually. In the oldest known Carmelite Constitutions, those of the 1281 Chapter of London, seven annual communion days are established. Again, that indicates that some, if not many, of the brothers were not receiving communion even several times a year.

Furthermore, the *Pattern for Life* that Albert gave the hermits required the hermits to "solemnly hear" Mass each day when possible. That indicates they had to be present at Mass, but it also indicates that the liturgy was not a simple "low Mass" but a liturgy celebrated with some solemnity. Indeed the hermits seem to have used the Jerusalem liturgy which was a rather elaborate liturgy with many exotic feasts such as the "Going of Noah into the Ark" and the "Exit of Noah from the Ark," feasts that pitiably do not show up in the more sober Roman Rite, much to its lacklustre. The liturgy would have required some work on the part of the hermits with its chants and lessons and the required ceremonial. In the event, their chapel was rather small but certainly adequate for their needs.

A note should be made that while the hermits did not say the Divine Office–as the majority were laity they did not need too–their prayer life in their cells revolved around the psalms appointed for the office. This is a bit of a curiosity. Many lay hermit groups simply had an "Our Father Office" such as the one appointed in the *Way of Life* for those who could not read. Others repeated simple ejaculatory prayers several dozen–or even several hundred–times accompanied by prostrations or genuflections. Still others, presumably groups that had numbers of priests and clerics among their number, did celebrate the Divine Office in common. Praying the psalms throughout the course of the day had long been a monastic practice–it had been the heart of the life of the desert monks back as far the third and fourth centuries. But it is a curious invention to make the ongoing prayer the psalms, not any psalms but the psalms appointed for the Divine Office, and yet not require the Office itself. Again, it may indicate that there were a number of priests and clerics in the first community, men who would have had to pray the Office anyway, and the other hermits were just following suit with what they could do without breviaries. On the other hand, if there was any concentration of clerics, they probably would have insisted on praying the Office together which was the norm–even for secular priests–in the thirteenth century. The requirement of the psalms without the Office itself is just a curiosity, and in fact even before the 1230's, a good decade and a half before Innocent IV would require the Divine Office to be said, the solitary recitation of the psalms would have begun to slip away in favour of the practice of the common Office prayed in choir. What is important, the bottom line of the matter, is that the heart of their prayer was the psalms. Albert's prescription of the psalms was a good scriptural prayer, requiring the psalms to be memorized and stored in the mind and heart, and it provided the foundation for a sound spirituality not merely pious practices.

The Letter

Sometime between his arrival in the Holy Land in 1206 and his death in 1214, the Patriarch Albert wrote a letter to the hermits spelling out the *Pattern for Life* to which he saw them called. It would seem that the hermits had approached the Patriarch and asked him for his blessing and guidance. Moreover, as already said, it would seem that they presented a proposal to him as to how he should constitute them as a community of lay hermits under his protection. In the event, he far surpassed their proposal. His vision for them was far wider than that which they had seen for themselves.

Although Albert did not intend to give the hermits a formal Rule–they were not Regulars, after all–but a

Formula Vitae or *Pattern for Life*, a letter was an often used procedure for such a charter. First of all, we should understand the difference between a *Formula Vitae,* a *Pattern for Life,* and a Rule. Some scholars make too much of a difference in this, but nevertheless, is there an important distinction. Those who follow a Rule (in Latin, a *Regula*) become *Regulars*–that is Religious. Albert was not trying to make our lay hermits anything more than lay hermits, so he did not write a *Regula* for them. He gave them a document of lower standing in the canon law, a *Formula Vitae,* or a *Pattern for Life*. Now, again, I think we have to be careful here not to exaggerate the difference. Saint Clare, the foundress of the Poor Clares, also received not a *Regula* but a *Formula Vitae* for her nuns. Nevertheless, when Pope Innocent IV reissued Albert's *Formula Vitae* with changes he had mandated in 1247, it became a *Regula*, a Rule, because the lay hermits were now properly constituted canonical Religious.

There are Rules that are in letter form and Rules that are not in letter form. The Rule of Saint Benedict, the best known Rule in the Middle Ages, was not in letter form. Neither was the Rule of Saint Francis for his new community in letter form. This is notably strange because Francis' Rule was issued as a Papal Bull (letter) but was not in the classic format for such a letter. On the other hand, the Rule that Innocent III issued for John of Matha's Trinitarians was in letter form, as was the *Formula Vitae* given to Saint Clare. So Rules can come in letter form or not.

Kees Waijman from the Dutch Province of Carmelites has done some extensive study on the *Formu-*

lae Vitae of Albert for the hermits and the significance of it being in the format of a letter. At a Conference on the Rule in San Antonio Texas several years ago, Father Kees points out that a medieval letter had five parts.
1. the *salutatio* or greeting.
2. the *exordium* where the point of the letter is introduced
3. the *narattio* where the point of the letter is explained in detail
4. the *petitio* or petition where something concrete is asked by the sender of the recipient
5. the *conclusio* or conclusion

Father Kees showed how the letter Albert sent the hermits follows this classic pattern. If Kees is correct, and he certainly makes a strong argument for this theory, Albert's chief point will be found in the exordium.

Many and varied are the ways in which our saintly forefathers laid down how everyone, whatever his station or the kind of religious observance he has chosen, should live a life of allegiance to Jesus Christ – how, pure in heart and stout in conscience, he must be unswerving in the service of his Master. It is to me, however, that you have come for a Rule of life in keeping with your avowed purpose, a Rule you may hold fast to…

The point of Albert's letter as found in the *exordium*, then, is to call the hermits to live a life of allegiance to Jesus Christ. In the *narattio* Albert spelled out to them in some detail how they should live that life of allegiance to Christ. In this description, he incorporated their proposal to him, but he was to go far beyond their original proposal. Indeed, at the seminar on the Rule in Lisieux in 2005, the Irish Carmelite, Brother Patrick Mullins, established a crucial connection between Albert's exordium that the hermits live a life of allegiance to Jesus Christ and the following passage that is found in the *narattio*.

"Since man's life on earth is a time of trial, and all who would live devotedly in Christ must undergo persecution, and the devil your foe is on the prowl like a roaring lion looking for prey to devour, you must use every care to clothe yourselves in God's armour so that you may be ready to withstand the enemy's ambush. Your loins are to be girt with chastity, your breast fortified by holy meditations, for, as Scripture has it, holy meditation will save you. Put on holiness as your breastplate, and it will enable you to love the Lord your God with all your heart and soul and strength, and your neighbour as yourself. Faith must be your shield on all occasions, and with it you will be able to quench all the flaming missiles of the wicked one: there can be no pleasing God without faith; [and the victory lies in this – your faith]. On your head set the helmet of salvation, and so be sure of deliverance by our only Saviour, who sets his own free from their sins. The Sword of the Spirit, the Word of God, must abound in your mouths and hearts. Let all you do have the Lord's Word for accompaniment."

But before we explore this in any detail, let us first look at Albert's contribution and examine how he saw the hermits and their role.

How the Bishop saw the Hermits

Again, it is difficult to know with any certainty how much of the Rule was in the hermits' original proposal and how much was Albert's contribution, but Craig Morrison's work has certainly shown us when we can see Albert's hand at work. Before we look at Albert's writing, let us consider if the Patriarch himself was involved in the task or if he delegated it to his staff. He was after all a busy man. Patriarch and Papal Legate, important work occupied his time. One would think that he would be far too busy to have the leisure to write a *Formula Vitae* for a group of as yet insignificant hermits living in a mountain valley at the edge of the Crusader State. When the Umiliati had been organized into a Religious Order, some ten years before perhaps, and he was a mere archbishop, he was required only to chair a commission to provide them with a canonical way of life. Certainly this business with the hermits is something that his staff could attend to. And yet, surprisingly, the finished product is such a harmonious work of spiritual doctrine that it is almost certainly the work of a single author, and one of exceptional spiritual maturity and insight. Furthermore, the insight of Doctor Mullins about the meaning of the phrase in the *exordium* "our saintly forefathers" indicates that the author was himself a Canon Regular of the Holy Cross of Mortara for Mullins claims that the phrase refers to the Rule of that community to which Albert himself belonged and which was known as the Rule of the Holy Fathers, referring to the Fathers of the Church, Saints Augustine, Jerome, Gregory the Great, Prosper of Aquitaine, and Isidore of Seville, whose writings were cited in this Rule. Finally, the mission which Albert set for the hermits in the *exordium* and its corresponding passage in what is now chapters 18 and 19 of the Rule is a mission that no one less than the Patriarch could give them. In other words, I think it is very likely that Albert took the time away from his many duties and wove the hermits' proposal into a mission statement of great depth and broad scope. Let's look at those parts of the Rule that show Albert's handiwork.

Albert, called by God's favour to be Patriarch of the Church of Jerusalem, bids health in the Lord and the blessing of the Holy Spirit to his beloved sons in Christ, B. and the other hermits under obedience to him, who live near the spring on Mount Carmel.

Many and varied are the ways in which our saintly predecessors laid down how everyone, whatever one's station or the kind of religious observance one has chosen, should live a life of allegiance to Jesus Christ–how pure in heart and stout in conscience, we must be unswerving in the service of our Master. It is to me, however, that you have come for a Rule of life in keeping with your avowed purposes, a Rule you may hold fast to henceforward; and therefore:

Each one of you is to stay in your own cell or nearby, pondering the Lord's law day and night and keeping watch at your prayers unless attending to some other duty.

None of you must lay claim to anything as your own, but your property is to be held in common; and of such things as the Lord may have given you each is to receive from the Prior–that is from the one the prior appoints for this purpose– whatever befits one's particular age and needs. However, as I have said, each one of you is to stay in your allotted cell, and live by yourself on what is given out to you.

Since our life on earth is a time of trial, and all who would live devotedly in Christ must undergo persecution, and the devil your foe is on the prowl like a roaring lion looking for prey to devour, you must use every care to clothe yourselves in God's armour so that you may be ready to withstand the enemy's ambush. Your loins are to be girt with chastity, your breast fortified by holy meditations, for as Scripture has it, holy meditation will save you. Put on holiness as your breastplate, and it will enable you to love the Lord your God with all your heart and soul and strength, and your neighbour as yourself. Faith must be your shield on all occasions, and with it you will be able to quench all the flaming arrows of the wicked one: there can be no pleasing God without faith; and the victory lies in this–your faith, On your head set the helmet of salvation and so be sure of deliverance by our only Saviour, who sets his own free from their sins. The Sword of the Spirit, the Word of God, must abound in your mouths and hearts. Let all you do have the Lord's Word for accompaniment.

You must give yourselves to work of some kind, so that the devil may always find you busy; no idleness on our part must give him a chance to pierce the defences of your souls. In this respect you have both the teaching and the example of Saint Paul the

Apostle, into whose mouth Christ put his own words. God made him preacher and teacher of faith and truth to the nations: with him as your leader you cannot go astray We lived among you, he said, labouring and weary, toiling night and day so as not to be a burden to any of you; not because we had no power to do otherwise but so as to give you, in our own selves, an example you might imitate, for the charge we have given you when we were with you was this: that whoever is not willing to work should not be allowed to eat either. For we have heard that there are certain restless idlers among you. We charge people of this kind, and implore them in the name of our Lord Jesus Christ, that they earn their own bread by silent toil.

The apostle would have us keep silence, for in silence he tells us to work. As the Prophet also makes known to us: Silence is the way to foster holiness. Elsewhere he says: Your strength will lie in silence and hope. For this reason I lay down that you are to keep silence from Vespers until Terce the next day, unless some necessary or good reason, or the prior's permission, should break the silence. At other times although you need not keep silence so strictly, be careful not to indulge in a great deal of talk, for as Scripture has it–and experience teaches us no less–sin will not be wanting where there is much talk and whoever is careless in speech will come to harm; and elsewhere; the use of many words brings harm to the speaker's soul. And our Lord says in the Gospel: Every vain word uttered will have to be accounted for on judgment day. Make a balance then, each of you, to weigh your words in; keep a tight rein on your mouths, lest you should stumble and fall in speech, and your fall be irreparable and prove mortal. Like the Prophet, watch your step lest your tongue give offense, and employ every care in keeping silent, which is the way to foster holiness.

You, Brother B. and whoever may succeed you as Prior, must always keep in mind and put into practice what Our Lord said in the Gospel: Whoever has a mind to become leader among you must become servant to the rest, and whichever of you would be first must become your bondsman.

You others hold your Prior in humble reverence, your minds not on the individual but on Christ who has placed your Prior over you, and who, to those who rule the Churches, addressed the words: Whoever pays you heed pays heed to me, and whoever treats you with dishonour dishonours me; if you remain so minded you will not be found guilty of contempt, but will merit life eternal as fit reward for your obedience.

Here then are the few points I have written down to provide you with a standard of conduct to live up to: but Our Lord, at his second coming, will reward anyone who does more than obligation demands. See that the bounds of common sense are not exceeded however, for common sense is the guide of the virtues.

Now, again, there is no clear way of knowing for sure what is Albert's contribution and what is the hermits', but the above passages are either clearly Albert's work (his greeting for example) or show the very sophisticated ways in which Albert used the scriptures to bring forth his arguments. Beneath some of Albert's scriptural arguments there may well be bits and pieces of the original hermit proposal–requiring work for example, or silence–but they have been so overlaid with Albert's biblical style that their rewriting must be considered his. We will comment on the various parts of the passage when we look at the text chapter by chapter, but what I want to point out now is the link between "a life of allegiance to Jesus Christ" in the *exordium* and the idea of spiritual warfare that surfaces later in the *narratio* of the text.

Brother Patrick Mullins in the paper he presented at Lisieux made it clear that when Albert introduces the theme that the hermits are to live a life of allegiance to Jesus Christ they are swearing service to him as knights swear to serve their Lord, and they in turn are expecting something from their Lord–*salus* is the Latin word the Albert uses later in his *Formula Vitae*, a word that means both safety and salvation. When a knight swore fealty to a lord he pledged to fight for the lord, but the lord in turn promised the knight protection and safety for himself, his lands, and his family. And so these hermits are to be spiritual knights, sworn in the service of the Lord of lords, and he in turn will provide them with their eternal safety, their eternal protection. Albert tells his hermits that the real battle, the real enemy, is not flesh and blood. The enemy is not Saladin and armies. The real battle is with the Evil One who wages eternal warfare against God and his saints.

Albert undoubtedly saw the failure of the Crusades. After a century and more of fighting and battles, the Land still did not belong to Christ. The Muslims once again held Jerusalem. The Christians had been unable to hold the land they had won, and while they were able to regain a part during the third crusade, their hold was tenuous. They had not won the hearts of the people, even the Christian population. They were only a few thousand knights against the vast Arab armies. Perhaps Albert was discouraged that he could not even get to his own Patriarchal Cathedral, now behind enemy lines. They had fought the wrong war. They had thought the enemy was Islam and they had thought the weapons were violence and terror. And it was not successful. It was time for a new Crusade, a new battle, the true battle–the battle with evil. Albert gave the hermits a mission: to succeed where the knights had failed. They were called to fight, not with swords and lances and catapults, but with the armour and weapons of God. To wage a war of holiness, a battle of sanctity, knowing that righteousness will prevail in the sight of God and thus that justice will win where violence has failed. This then was Albert's vision for his hermits.

The Church and the need for change

The hermits found themselves in a Church that was not very different from the Church today in some respects. A very innovative pope, Innocent III, had opened the door to a period of experimentation and reform to help the Church adjust to the massive social changes of the time. Europe was evolving from localized rural cultures to a busy urban and commercial international society. As more and more people moved to the cities from the countryside, found work, established businesses, and increased trade a strong middle class emerged and political power shifted more and more to this middle class from the old nobility. Indeed, we should be careful about the term middle class, as some of these "new families" were wealthy–often far wealthier than the old noble families. The sons of these new families, because they were not noble, were not eligible to become knights. Instead they studied law at the universities that were springing up all over Europe. They then entered the service of their various kings and wielded tremendous power in government, in society, and in the Church.

This new urban wealthy and middle class society presented numerous problems for the Church. The traditional monastic life was centred in rural abbeys. The young men from the new urban families did not feel drawn to the rural monastic life. Furthermore, the abbeys themselves were used to taking only the sons or daughters of the nobility and did not want vocations from these *noveau riche* merchant families. And in the cities, there were too few parishes and too few priests to accommodate the rapidly growing population. As a result, the new working and middle class families often felt very alienated from the Church. Various heretical or schismatic groups began making serious inroads among the new citizens and drawing them away from the Church.

Innocent III was a forward looking pope who was willing to search for new solutions and not afraid to try ideas that were new and sometimes quite different than the past. He encouraged a variety of movements among the laity and even was willing to allow lay people an opportunity to speak in Church about their faith and what it meant to follow Jesus in the complex world of their day. He founded a variety of new Religious Orders, in fact new types of Religious Orders. He was a great admirer of Saint Francis and gave his blessing to the lay hermits who gathered around Francis as his first "lesser brothers," the Friars Minor. He also gave his blessing to Saint John of Matha who organized a new community of priests and brothers who would raise money for the ransom of captives held by the Muslims in the Crusades. He reconciled several schismatic groups to the Church, even forming Religious communities out of them. With one such group, the Umiliati, he affiliated their lay members to the Religious in the first "Third Order." Innocent was a canon lawyer, but he was one who did not see the law as restrictive of new ways but rather used the canon law to support his experimental ideas.

Not everyone was happy with all the experimentation that Innocent was allowing. There was tremendous change in the Church and there are always those for whom change causes anxiety. Towards the end of his pontificate, Innocent called an Ecumenical Council to meet at the Lateran Basilica in Rome and the bishops felt that it was time to regulate things a bit more closely. The Fourth Lateran Council passed many of the laws of the Church that we still follow today, such as the requirement for Communion during the Easter Season and annual confession. They also defined the number of the sacraments at seven, naming them as we have them today in the Church. Most dramatically the bishops said that no new Religious Orders were to be founded. More precisely what they meant was that no new Rules were to be given and that new communities should choose an approved Rule. Fortunately for us Carmelites, our Rule had been given by the Patriarch Albert previous to this restriction, although the Carmelites would have to defend their right to exist for most of the thirteenth century.

One of the results of the Council was that the new Religious communities began conforming more closely to the canon law. Lay groups such as the Franciscans and the Carmelites knew that they had to become Religious and over the next several decades began making changes in their Rules and in their customs that made them conform to the canon law. Little by little they began moving from their status as lay hermits to mendicant friars, a status which the Church was beginning to acknowledge as a new and approved form of Religious Life. Vows of poverty and chastity had to be added to their Rules so that they would have the three vows of religion. Certain issues regarding poverty had to be addressed. Their relationship with the local bishop and with the Papacy as well as their rights and privileges had to be more clearly defined. In the case of the Carmelites a series of papal bulls from 1226 until 1247 gradually introduced a variety of these changes.

Also the need of the Church for priests to preach and hear confessions increased pressure on these new communities to have more and more of their men ordained. The frequently-given permission for lay hermits to preach was gradually withdrawn and it was required that a man be a priest or deacon to preach. At the same time, the communities themselves relocated from the poor shanty-towns and rural slums outside the cities where they were most often located and established churches and houses in the city where they could more effectively minister to the people. The new mendicant communities began sending more of their men to university to study so that they could teach good theology to their students and preach well to the people. The increased clericalization also made changes in their lifestyle. Clerics were obligated to the Divine Office, which until the sixteenth century was normally prayed publicly in the Church. As more and more of the Carmelites were ordained they began praying the Divine Office in choir instead of the psalms in their cells. Finally in 1247 Pope Innocent IV required two Dominicans, Cardinal Hugh of Saint Cher and Bishop William of Tortosa, to examine the *Pattern for Life* which Albert had given the hermits and make it conform to the canon law so that the hermits might be canonical Religious. With this change, Albert's *Formula Vitae* becomes a proper *Regula*, that is the *Pattern for Life* became the Rule. The lay hermits become Religious.

An Enthusiasm for the Gospel

One of the most interesting characteristics of the twelfth and thirteenth centuries, a characteristic that

The background

created the possibility for the emergence of the new Religious communities such as the Carmelites and Franciscans, was a popular enthusiasm for the Gospel. As the cities of Europe came back to life in eleventh and twelfth centuries and the rural population swarmed in looking for jobs, finding not only employment but financial success and emerging into a new middle class, more and more ordinary people had both the time and education to read. Books were incredibly expensive, of course, being copied by hand. Bibles were rare and very expensive. But religious books, replete with bible stories, were common enough. And of course, the newly constructed churches were being filled with stained glass and sculpture that depicted bible stories. Preachers related biblical stories that captured the minds–and hearts–of their listeners. And wealthy merchants often paid priests to prepare translations of the Gospels into the popular language they could understand. But this enthusiasm was not simply to know the biblical story or read the Gospel. People wanted to translate their religious faith into concrete action. People of means took seriously the biblical injunction to store up treasure in heaven and gave generously to institutions that served the poor. Wealthy women took time to organize charities for orphans and widows. Men formed confraternities to assist the sick or the lame. A wealthy merchant by the name of Peter Waldo, hearing the Gospel "if you be perfect, go sell all that you have, give to the poor so you will have treasure in heaven, then come and follow me" took to the words to heart. He went home from Mass, paid dowries to put his daughters in a fashionable convent with royal connections, turned his business over to his wife, gave away all his cash, left his home and family, and began preaching in the streets as a poor man. People joined him, forming communities whose members shared their meagre belongings and who preached the poverty of Christ and the apostles as a model of life. Unfortunately, the Church was not prepared to deal with lay people who were taking the Gospel more seriously than the clergy, and Waldo and his followers were excommunicated. But with the election of Innocent III, the Church learned from this mistake in not taking Waldo's Gospel convictions seriously and when a young son of a wealthy Assisi cloth merchant did likewise, the Church took him under its protection and he eventually became a saint. Thousands flocked to him too as people wanted to follow Christ and Francis offered a way. When Francis was asked to provide a Rule for his followers, he answered that the Gospel was Rule enough. It wasn't enough, of course, for the canon lawyers, but Francis made sure that his disciples knew that their vocation would be found in the following of Christ and his Gospel more than in any other text.

Francis and is followers were not alone in this determination to follow the Gospel. The imitation of Christ energized lay and clerical spirituality of the period. It motivated lay hermits, pilgrims, monks, beguines, penitents, and countless ordinary Christians. The wealthy and the middle class gave time to work in hospitals, care for lepers, collect the homeless off the street and shelter them, look after orphans, protect widows, assist the elderly–all in the name of the

Gospel. Jesus was a living presence for many of these people and when they heard his Gospel they responded with concrete action. The Gospel was a strong force in people's lives. It was a time that people received communion rarely–often only once a year–and was just before the Church introduced the practices of Eucharistic adoration on a popular level. Thus the Gospel was the main contact people had with Christ and it produced some tremendous results. Not everyone became committed to a living faith, of course, but the twelfth and thirteenth centuries are often seen as one of the great peaks of Catholic life and devotion and this period took its energy from the Gospel in a way that previous–and, alas, subsequent–centuries seem not to have.

By the end of the thirteenth century there was a huge emphasis in the Church on doctrine whereas at the beginning it seems to have been more on practice. Much of the energy of the later Middle Ages would be channelled into devotional practices more than works of charity. The new Religious communities which had been so evangelical became more and more structured and part of the social and religious institutions of the day. Charity certainly did not grow cold. Most of the charitable confraternities lasted to the Protestant Reformations and some even to the French Revolution, but the enthusiasm for the Gospel slowly all but burned itself out. After the Council of Trent and the Catholic Reformations, doctrine and dogma shaped Catholic life more than the Gospels and Catholics often knew their faith well but the bible very little. Nevertheless, in Carmel the seeds of the evangelical renewal in which the Order had been born continued. The great Carmelite mystics from John and Teresa down to Thérèse and Elizabeth of the Trinity all drew their inspiration from the scriptural texts. Thérèse is said to have known the Gospels practically by heart, and she had a great love for the prophets as well. Elizabeth is amazingly Pauline in her spirituality–all the more amazing when one considers how little exposure she had to biblical theology or theology in general. The Gospel remains at the heart of Carmelite spirituality and, thanks to the Rule of Saint Albert and its emphasis on scripture, always will.

The move to Europe

Much of the pressure for the Carmelites to change came from their move to Europe. Beginning in about 1238, groups of the hermits began migrating back to Europe. They went to Messina in Sicily. In 1242 they came to Aylesford in England and Hulne in Northumberland. They came to France. And from these first foundations they spread out across Italy and Britain and the Low Countries to Germany and Ireland and Scotland. While they were never as popular as the Franciscans or Dominicans, or even the Augustinians for that matter, they did grow quite rapidly. Most of the recruits who joined them had never been to Mount Carmel. Most likely many of them never understood the eremitical life. The situation in Europe with its flourishing cities was quite different than the situation on Mount Carmel. Seeing the work the Franciscans

The background

and Dominicans were doing in the cities and towns of Europe, many Carmelites began to be anxious to undertake a more apostolic life as well. The pastoral needs of the people were there and the needs were real. Furthermore, the pastoral ministry brought in needed income to help the new communities build their churches and priories. The lay eremitical life was vanishing in Europe as pope and bishops alike wanted lay hermits to become proper Religious. It was inevitable that the Carmelites should evolve into something quite different than they had been. In fact, had they not become mendicant friars, available to serve the pastoral needs of the people, they may well have been among the many Religious orders that the Second Ecumenical Council of Lyons suppressed in 1274. As it was, the Augustinians and Carmelites barely escaped suppression, and then only because they were "useful" to the needs of the Church, a category in which they most likely would not have been classified had they remained lay hermits.

A Voice of Protest

Change is never easy, but it is inevitable. Cardinal Newman wrote in the nineteenth century: "in a higher world it is otherwise, but here below to live is to change, and to be perfect is to have changed often." Some people, however, resist change. The voice of resistance surfaced in Carmel in a letter which most scholars still believe was written just before the Council of Lyons by the then-Prior General, Nicholas Gallicus. The letter is entitled the *Ignea Saggita*, the "Fiery Arrow." At first read it seems to be an acrimonious indictment of those members of the Order who wanted the change from the eremitical to the mendicant life, but when one reads it carefully it is a brilliant defence of the contemplative life itself. Very honestly, the letter may well date from a later period of the Order's history when friars were seeking a reform that would reorient them towards the contemplative life rather than be an indictment against the introduction of the mendicant life in the mid-thirteenth century. The text merits a scholarly attention it has yet to receive. But taking it at face value, it would tell us that not all the hermits wanted to become friars. There were some still attached to the simple life of the lay hermit. They believed that the greatest service they could render the Church was not in the pastoral field, but in the example they gave of lives of simple prayer in their hermitages. This letter, whether from the time when the Order was moving into the cities and undertaking pastoral ministry, or from a later period when Carmelites were calling for a return to the contemplative life of its first days, sets a tone to our spiritual writing that continues to value the desert ideals even when we are living in the realities of the city. The Carmelite, as deeply involved in ministry as he or she may be, must always be a hermit at heart. This does not mean that we Carmelites must have a romantic attachment to the eremitical life, but rather that we must find the interior desert within our soul and the cell of the deepest chamber of our heart and draw our strength from that centre rather than from the energy we spend in our busy and active lives. The Carmelite values silence and solitude while giving himself, or herself, over to whatever God calls us to in the moment. The busiest apostle can still be a hermit, the desert and the hermitage is a state of consciousness and a spiritual discipline, not a physical place.

Clericalization

One of the most notable changes in the hermits' *Pattern for Life* as they returned to Europe was that more and more of them sought to become priests. This was true in other lay movements as well as the Church pushed them more and more into more highly organized forms of Religious Life. In part this was due to the need the Church had for priests in the 13th century with the rapidly growing population in the cities. There were needs for preachers and confessors as well as for churches where the people could attend Mass. It also gave the Church a greater measure of control over the lay movements however as once their members started being ordained, there were more canon laws that governed the way they lived.

For the Carmelite hermits as they returned to Europe and felt the pressure to clericalize–that is to become a Religious Order composed primarily of clerical and priestly members rather than a community of lay brothers–there were changes to be made in the way they lived. The most notable of these was that as clerics they were obligated not merely to recite the psalms that Albert had told them to pray, but to pray the Divine Office itself. In the Middle Ages, priests and clerics did not pray the Office privately as most do today. It was normal even for diocesan priests to pray the Office standing before the altar in the church as a liturgical act. And so our Carmelites slowly began in the 1230's and 1240's to gather in their chapels or in the new churches the bishops entrusted to them and pray the Office together. They brought back with them from the Holy Land some fairly novel ceremonies and strange feasts, but these only made them more of a popular curiosity. They developed their own Rite for the Office and the Mass and did not follow the Roman Rite that was more frequently followed in the Church in Europe.[4] They established a strong tradition of praying the Office in common, a tradition which persists to the present day and which since Vatican II is shared by the Lay Carmelites as well.

Another change made by the hermits as they clericalized was that they realized they had a need for a better

---

[4] Actually before the Council of Trent and the Missal of Pius V there were a tremendous variety of rites in the Church and many Religious Orders, not just the Carmelites, had their unique rite. Many dioceses or ecclesiastical regions also had their own particular rite. The development of a uniform western rite is quite late. The Discalced Carmelites adopted the Roman Rite very early in their history, but the Carmelite Order itself retained its own Rite until after the Second Vatican Council when it adopted the *Missale Romanum* issued by Pope Paul VI in 1969. Both the Discalced Carmelites and the Carmelite Order still have unique features to their liturgy such as their proper calendars of saints and the propers and prefaces for many of the feasts which are celebrated in the Orders, but there is no permission any longer to use the pre-Vatican II Rite.

education. If they were to preach and hear confessions they had to be prepared for this ministry and so they began sending their brighter students off to the universities of Europe to study theology. The Carmelites never became as scholarly as the Dominicans, or even the Franciscans, but they did produce a fair number of Doctors over the years and several of them achieved some renown in the scholarly world. Scholarship continues to be important to Carmel today as well and in the modern world there is a need not only for theology and biblical studies, but for a wide variety of academic disciplines.

An unfortunate consequence of clericalization was that very shortly a two tiered system emerged in which the non-clerical brothers lost an active role in decision making in the community. The priests and clerics were given the privileges and power, the "lay-brothers" were expected, for the most part, to do the manual labour and not to complain. By the fourteenth century there was a further concentration of power and only those with the doctorate in Theology were allowed to be superiors or to attend the General Chapters of the Order. This created an unfortunate aristocracy in the Order, very different than the original fraternal spirit. In the Carmelites, the priests and brothers always wore the same habit, and until the 17th century used the same title–"Fra" or Brother. Today, in more and more places, Carmelite priests are going back to the title "Brother" rather than "Father" and the brothers have been able to take leadership roles again, though the Holy See still does not allow them to be major superiors. That will probably change in the next few decades. Indeed some of our finest theologians and writers are not ordained. Within the community itself there is no distinction of privilege or status between priests and brothers since Vatican II.

Poverty

An essential part of the hermit vocation was a special type of poverty that included the renunciation of both individual and communal wealth. Unlike the Religious Orders of the day in which the individual Religious renounced the right to own property but the community itself often held extensive lands and properties as well as beautiful churches and monasteries, the evangelical groups that emerged in the 13th century wanted to imitate Christ and his apostles in their total poverty. They looked to a stirring comment from Saint Jerome, the fourth century biblical scholar, and attempted to *nudus nudum Christum sequi*–to naked follow the naked Christ. They wanted to give up not only "brothers, sisters, children, parents" to follow Christ, but "houses and lands" as well. Thus they renounced any ownership, even of the land on which they lived and the buildings that sheltered them. They refused any fixed income or investments and determined to live by their manual labour and by begging alms. In choosing this radical approach to poverty they had an amazing effect on the society of their day as people expressed their admiration for their commitment and as vocations flocked to the new communities that asked so much in the decision to follow Jesus.

An important aspect of this commitment was the decision to hold whatever they did have–whatever food they gathered, clothing they obtained, poor furnishings in their houses, books for prayer and study–not as individuals but in common. They wanted to imitate the Jerusalem community of the Acts of the Apostles who held all things in common. They were, in fact, communists. When we hear "communist," we think Marxist or Leninist and it is a negative term, but Christian communism has been practiced by various groups in the Church since the New Testament. The various hermit groups of the 13th century, including the Latin hermits on Mount Carmel, were very committed to this principle of renouncing private ownership and sharing whatever resources God blessed them with.

Vatican II and the Laity

In 1959 the newly elected Pope, John XXIII, surprised the world in announcing that he was calling all the bishops of the Church to Rome for a particular type of meeting that is held only rarely in the history of the Church, an Ecumenical Council. John announced that the goal of this Council was to prepare a new period in the Church's history, a time in which he hoped that it would be possible to reconcile the many divisions into which Christianity had fallen through the centuries. To do this, John admitted, would require a renewal and even reform of the Catholic Church itself. Few people at the time, even the good pope himself, probably realized just how thorough a renewal and reform would be required.

There were those, especially in Rome, who were very opposed to a Council. The last Council, Vatican I, had in 1870 declared the Pope to be infallible and to have full authority to govern the Church. There was, in their mind, no need for a Council. The Pope could simply decree whatever changes he saw fit. But Pope John knew that this was part of the problem. If the wounds of Christianity were to be healed, then the chief shepherd on earth of the Church had to be a servant not a dictator. It was in gathering and empowering his brother bishops, the pope realized, that reform and renewal was most likely to happen. Even so, no one expected the bishops to be quite as vociferous in the reform and renewal of the Church as they were.

The Pope's advisors in Rome, the various prelates of the Curia, spent the two-and-a-half years before the Council preparing all the documents they thought would be necessary. They drew up documents with innocuous phrases that sounded lovely but in fact changed very little. When the bishops finally gathered, in the autumn of 1962, they looked at the draft documents and declared them totally unsuitable. They wanted real change, not just window-dressing. The Council Fathers, then, with the encouragement of Pope John, formed committees and commissions to undertake a far more radical self-examination of the Church than the Roman officials had wanted. They met each autumn from 1962 until 1965. At the end of the Council, the Church understood itself and its mission in very different ways than it had before the Council began.

We cannot look at all the changes of the Council as we examine the Rule of Saint Albert and its impact on Lay Carmelites. There is much that does not pertain to our study. But we certainly want to look at how Vatican II envisioned the role of the laity. In the years after Vatican I, a number of English Churchmen had been asked what they saw the role of the laity to be. One of them, a Monsignor Talbot, said that the role of the Laity was "to hunt, to shoot, and to entertain." Obviously all the laity the Monsignor knew were of the gentry class. He didn't consider the Irish maid who brought him his tea or the butler who brushed his hat to be of much use to the Church. Cardinal Newman, on the other hand, said that he wasn't quite sure what the role of the laity was, but "that the Church would look foolish without them." The controversy had actually started when Newman wrote an article entitled "On Consulting the Faithful in Matters of Doctrine." While this article had brought immense displeasure on Newman at the time, his views prevailed at Vatican II. The Council looked at the laity as an essential nucleus of the Church and not merely some appendage that was expected to silently follow without question. Indeed, the Council identified two crucial aspects of the lay vocation. One is that the laity, like everyone else in the Church and to the same degree as everyone else in the Church, is called to holiness. The second is that it is the laity, not the clergy, who are to represent the Church in the public realm–politics, economics, the secular sciences and education. The clergy are to confine themselves to the Gospel, the laity take the Gospel into the modern world.

These two facets have important impact for the role of the Laity in Carmel.

There is no hierarchy of holiness in *Lumen Gentium*, the Dogmatic Constitution of the Church published by the Council. Priests are not more holy than married people, nor Religious more holy than single people. Though the vocations differ and the expressions of spirituality within those vocations will differ, the holiness to which we are all called is the same perfection of Charity. This is a remarkable step away from the old catechism in which we were taught that the Religious Life, for example, was more perfect than the married life. This has empowered us to reassert our claim for Carmel to be a family. The Nuns, the Friars, Hermits, laity, Religious Sisters all express the charism of Carmel in different ways and with different emphases, but the core vocation to holiness is the same for all. The Religious are not more Carmelite than the laity. The life of the Nuns is not more holy than the married life of Lay Carmelites. Individuals may be more holy within their particular vocation but that is due to their cooperation with the grace offered them, not because of the vocation itself. The dispute about the Rule of Saint Albert and the laity, at least to a certain extent, is a dispute about this point.

The second point to consider is the role of the laity as representing the Church in the secular forum. Just as the laity are called to be the voice of the Church in the secular arena of life, so too the Laity of the Order are called to be the voice of Carmel in the world. This is an area where both the Church and Order have fallen far short of the potential. The first thing needed to do is to prepare the Laity with good education and formation to represent the Church, or in our case the Order, in the public arena. The NGO at the United Nations is one such forum in which the Carmelite Laity should be empowered to act on behalf of the Order. Lay Carmelites should be visible, as Carmelites, in other public *fora* as well. But this requires both sound theological education and good Carmelite formation before these roles can be appropriately filled. It is an embarrassment to the Order when a Carmelite, Religious or lay, stands up and gives an opinion which is ill-informed. When we speak as Carmelites we represent the Order and we must present not our personal opinions but the view of the Carmelite Order. Many of the issues facing us today in the Church and in society are very complex issues. Many Catholics think they know what the Church teaches about some very complicated subjects ranging from stem-cell research to international peace but, in fact, miss essential nuances in Church teaching. They claim to speak for the Church when they in fact do not. The *World Wide Web* is filled with "Catholic Sites" that claim orthodoxy but speak without any ecclesiastical backing and misrepresent Church teaching. The challenge ahead of the Church is to provide sound theological education for those who would speak in its name. When one speaks for the Order it is even more complex. One must be in theological harmony with the Church, for the Order must speak in concert with magisterium, but one also must know the Carmelite tradition very well. This means ongoing formation is always a priority for our Carmelites, Religious and Lay alike.

The Rule of Saint Albert and the Carmelite Laity

There is much debate in the Order about the relationship of the Carmelite Laity to the Rule of Saint Albert. A small and, at first, seemingly insignificant point of view surfaced at an international meeting of leaders in the Lay Carmelite movement at Fatima in Portugal in September, 1998 when the English speaking delegates at the conference asked why the Carmelite Laity should have a different "Rule" than the rest of the Carmelite family. The question had been bandied about among the English-speakers, beginning with the Australians, for several years before it was raised at Fatima, but the question sparked controversy when it was raised internationally.

Implicit in the question about whether the Third Order should have a separate Rule is a certain understanding of what it means to be a Carmelite, what it means to be a Religious or a layperson, and what is the relationship of the Carmelite Laity to the Religious of the Order. A further issue imbedded even more deeply pertains to the hierarchical nature of the Church and how the Order should reflect, or deflect, the hierarchical structures.

The Rule of Saint Albert as modified by Pope Innocent IV has long served as a document descriptive of life in Carmel. Indeed, when Albert gave the Rule to the hermit community on Mount Carmel, he called it a *Formula Vitae,* a "Way of Life" or a "Pattern for Life." The Rule, in its very simple prescriptions and moving exhortations, describes a way of life that Albert, on behalf of the Church, called the hermits to live. In many of its particulars that Albert's *Pattern for Life* no longer provides a literal description of life in Carmel. The conditions in which the Order has found itself historically has led to many of its clauses being reinterpreted as spiritual doctrine rather than as literal prescript. For example, while in the time of Albert Mass was invariably celebrated in the morning, and therefore Albert told the hermits that they should gather each morning to hear Mass, contemporary Carmelites often gather for the Eucharist in the late afternoon or in the evening, which works better for their schedules. A more substantial move away from a literalistic approach to the descriptive prescriptions of the Rule is requirement of abstinence from meat, a requirement not unsuited for the sedentary life of medieval hermits in Crusader Palestine who lived within sight of the sea. But when they moved to the cities of Europe, Carmelites found that a meatless diet did not give them the nourishment they needed for a busy apostolic life and that, if it meant providing fish or dairy to supplement their dietary needs, abstinence was often more costly that eating meat. Even before 1432 when the Holy See officially authorized a limited amount of meat to be served in the refectory, Carmelites had begun making the adjustments in their diet. But while meat has long been in the Carmelite diet, the general principle of some form of fast and abstinence remains an important part of the spiritual discipline of Carmel. The descriptive nature of the Rule is not to outline the particulars of a way of life, but to outline the values that constitute the spirituality of Carmel.

And this brings us to the second point, the Rule of Saint Albert is not only descriptive of Carmelite Life, but constitutive of Carmelite Life. That is to say, the Rule not only tells them how to live a Carmelite life, but declares that it is precisely in embracing this description of Carmelite life, or rather the spirituality and values of Carmelite life described in the Rule, that one becomes a Carmelite. Though the hermits had been living some sort of common life before they approached Albert for a Rule or *Formula Vitae*, it was only with the granting of that Rule that they became, in the eyes of the Church, an official community. Carmel only becomes Carmel when Albert bestows the *Formula Vitae* that portrays the unique spiritual vision that since has characterized it. Before he granted them his *Pattern of Life*, they were simply a collection of lay hermits without a particular identity. It is this document of Saint Albert that imparts the unique character we recognize as Carmelite, both by description and constitutional establishment, to the budding community. We receive our identity as Carmelites from embracing the Rule that has for eight centuries described and constituted us as Carmelites. Those who follow this Rule as the vision and path of their spiritual life are, at least in some sense, Carmelites. Those who do not look to this Rule for a pattern of Christian living–and there are certainly many other legitimate ways, as Albert himself points out, to follow Christ–are not Carmelites. This is the nub of the problem about the Rule and the laity. No one debates whether the Religious should look to the Rule as their *Pattern of Life*, the Religious know that their Carmelite identity comes from their bond to that text. But if the Laity too are not committed to the Rule of Saint Albert, are they truly Carmelite?

Sometimes the argument is advanced that since those hermits on Mount Carmel who approached Albert for a Rule were lay hermits, the Rule was actually written for Carmelite Laity. This argument is, of course, too good to be true. Yes the hermits were lay, in as that they were not monks or clerics. But in the twelfth and early thirteenth centuries, a time when many laypersons embraced the eremitical life, the divisions between laity and those who were not laity in the Church, was not so clear as it is today. Many men received clerical tonsure (making them clerics), but had not received the major orders (subdeacon, deacon, or priest) that required them to be celibate, leaving them free to marry and have secular employment. Furthermore, many men and women had come under the legal cloak of Mother Church in a variety of ambiguous status. For example Cistercian *conversi* or lay-brothers were not monks, but still enjoyed canonical status that legally separated them out from laymen. Anchorites, male and female, were often in a similar position. They were most usually not monks or nuns, but neither did they belong to the laity. Pilgrims who had taken up their quest with the blessing of the local bishop, were under the protection of the Church without losing their lay status. And so too were hermits who had sought canonical blessing and protection lay persons but of a special canonical status. Yes the hermits on Mount Carmel were lay, but once they had the blessing of the Church for their way of life, they stood in a different canonical relationship to the Church than other laity. So while these hermits were lay hermits, they were not lay people in the modern understanding of the Church. Today's Lay Carmelite stands in a different relationship to the Church than the lay hermit of the early thirteenth century.

More helpful for us to understand the importance of Albert's *Pattern for Life* to modern Carmelite Laity is the fact that as these hermits passed from the status of lay hermits to canonical Religious, and as more and more of them entered the clerical state, receiving Holy Orders, they began accepting members into their communities who very obviously were lay people and were not becoming Religious. In Italy, where they were particularly common, these Lay Carmelites were often called *pinzocheri* (male) or *pinzochere* (female). Some of them, were married, had families, and engaged in normal business leading lives very much immersed in the normal world of the laity, yet also had strong ties to the Friars and their communities. Some of them, however, were unmarried. The unmarried *pinzocheri* and *pinzochere*, often took vows and wore the Carmelite habit. In fact, we have the profession of vows of a married couple who became *pinzocheri* at the Carmelite Church of Florence. They lived separately, with the husband moving into the friary and the wife living, as did most of the professed *pinzochere*, in her private home nearby to the Carmelite Church. Other Orders, such as the Dominicans and Franciscans, had their *pinzocheri* as well. Saint Catherine of

Siena was a professed Dominican *pinzochera*, who wore the Dominican habit and went each day to the Dominican Church to pray, but who remained living in her family home.

Incidentally the only way a woman could become a Carmelite in the thirteenth and fourteenth centuries was to become a *pinzochera*. These *pinzochere,* although women, were affiliated to communities of Carmelite men. The first communities of Carmelite Nuns were only formed in 1452. The *pinzochere* of the Dominicans and Franciscans also, although those orders had monasteries of nuns, were affiliated to the Friars.

When these *pinzocheri* professed their vows, they professed them according to the same Rule as the Religious. There was no separate Rule for the Carmelite Laity at the time. There was only the Rule of Saint Albert as it had been modified by Pope Innocent IV in 1247. This Rule served both the Religious and the affiliated laity. And those laity who professed according to this Rule were very much seen as part of the family of Carmel.

Other Religious communities who affiliated the laity followed various practices. Saint Francis wrote a Rule for his Third Order and they have always had their own Rule. Laity affiliating to Benedictine houses as oblates, on the other hand, always took the Rule of Saint Benedict–the same Rule followed by the monks and nuns.

It was only in the reorganization of the Third Order by Prior General Theodore Straccio 1637 that the Third Order received its first 'Rule' distinct from the

Rule of Saint Albert.[5] This was in the context of the Reforms of the Council of Trent which emphasized, and perhaps can be said to have over-emphasized, the differences in the Church between the clergy and Religious, on one hand, and the Laity on the other. The lay state, and the holiness proper to it, was seen as less perfect than the vocations to the priesthood or Religious Life. This attitude dies hard even after Vatican II and its doctrine of the "Universal Call to Holiness." It has already been pointed out that the Second Vatican Council recognized the differences between the various vocations in the Church but did not rank them hierarchically as one being "more perfect" or "higher" than another. The Church has used the number of lay people who have been beatified and canonized since the Council to emphasize that sanctity is available to all in the Church without discrimination. Nevertheless, the prejudice against the lay vocation remains in subtle ways, sometimes clung too more strongly by Laity than by Religious. In the debate over the Rule, it was sometimes said that the Rule of Saint Albert was not for "simple laypeople," implying that the spirituality of the Rule requires a certain maturity suited only to the Religious. This prejudice dies hard. The current

---

[5] Blessed John Soreth had written a Rule in 1455 for a group of non-cloistered Carmelite Sisters–equivalent to today's Carmelite Religious Sisters. Similarly, Miguel de la Fuente wrote a Rule in 1624 for tertiaries who lived a semi-Religious life with public vows of chastity. But it was only in 1637 that the Third Order itself as a whole received a distinct Rule of their own.

Rule for the Third Order, Living the Carmelite Way, falls into this trap and refers to the Carmelite Laity as "Carmelites in a certain sense," implying that the Lay Carmelites are less members of the Order than the Religious. This "second-class" status for the Laity of the Order is not supported by either the historical roots of the Carmelite Laity or by our current documentation, except for the new Rule for the Third Order.

As was pointed out earlier, the issue of returning the Lay Carmelites to the Rule of Saint Albert surfaced at the 1998 meeting of the Carmelite Laity at Fatima. Those preparing this congress had a proposed a Third Order Rule which they thought would pass without opposition, but the English-speakers immediately raised the question whether instead of a separate Rule, the entire Order should be returned to the Rule of Saint Albert. A very lively discussion ensued and it was clear that the assembly was not ready to recommend any Rule for the Lay Carmelites. Whereas the English speakers were consistently opposed to a separate Rule, the Italians and Brazilians, along with the Donum Dei Missionary Family, expressed their convictions that the Religious and Laity should have separate Rules. The Spanish speakers were divided on the issue. All agreed that further study and dialogue were needed and the whole matter was remanded to the next Congress which would take place in Rome in 2001.

In the event, several Friars who championed a separate Rule for the Laity did not wait for further discussion but approached the Congregation for Institutes of the Consecrated Life and Societies of the Apostolic Life (formerly known as the Congregation for Religious) and solicited the opinion that the Rule of Saint Albert was for the Religious alone and that it was not proper for the Laity to follow the same Rule as the Friars, Nuns, and Religious Sisters. At the very same time, however the Discalced Carmelites, without any opposition from the Holy See, chose to put their Secular Order under the Rule of Saint Albert, leaving the humiliating impression that the Lay Carmelites were not capable of following the Rule of Saint Albert, but the Secular Discalced were.

When the delegates to the 2001 meeting arrived at the Carmelite Spiritual Centre in Sassone, outside Rome, they found that a Third Order Rule had been written and was waiting for their approval. Although Carmelite Laity in Spain and Italy had been shown the text and asked for their comments, the proposed Rule was not shown to the English-speaking Carmelites until they arrived in Rome for the 2001 meeting. Consequently there was no opportunity given for them to circulate the text among the Carmelite Laity in North America or other Anglophone provinces for their feedback and suggestions before the text was submitted for the approval of the delegates of the 2001 meeting. The final text reflects this lack of consultation and consequently fails to reflect the experience and insights of Carmelites in the English speaking sections of the Carmelite Family. The result is a document that, at least to Anglophone ears, falls flat and fails to inspire.

One of the chief defects of the new Third Order Rule is that, unlike the Rule of Saint Albert, it is not a "classic text." A "classic text" is a piece of literature–it does not have to be sacred literature–that is able to retain its depth of significance across the divisions of time and geography. A classic text speaks to people of many cultures and many periods of history. They may not all hear exactly the same thing from the text, but they all draw inspiration from it. The various interpretations that different cultures and historical settings give it each nuance it and, at least to some extent, complement one another in its interpretation. A "classic text" such as the *Confessions of Saint Augustine*, or the *Veni Creator Spiritus* would have meaning for a French nun in A.D. 1225, an Australian layman in 2007, and an African deacon in 2516. It may have different meanings, or suggest different ideas, to different people depending on what cultural experience they bring to it, but it has meaning in all situations. Shakespeare's *Romeo and Juliet* worked in London in 1615, in Philadelphia in 1910, in Kenya in 2000. It has inspired an Italian Opera and artwork from various countries. Similarly, Psalm 23 (The Lord is my Shepherd) is prayed by Protestants, Catholics, and Jews in every language used by believers, and even agnostics find comfort in it. Classic texts transcend the particularities of culture, of time, and of place.

The Rule of Saint Albert is such a classic text. It has inspired men and women for eight centuries and across the globe. We do not all understand or interpret it the same way. A score of major commentaries have been written on it over the centuries. Cloistered Nuns see things in it that apostolic Friars overlook. Hermits find inspiration in it as well as lay people. Carmelites from India will appreciate different aspects of it than Carmelites from Brazil. It challenges African Carmelites in different ways than it challenges American Carmelites. It offers depths of meaning, some shared meaning and some diverse meanings, to all its readers. It has "worked" for eight centuries and it will probably "work," please God many more centuries to come. But the Third Order Rules, both the current and previous, were not meant to function like that. They are more sets of guidelines. The rules and prescriptions they present are very bound to specific times and places in history. They become obsolete after ten or fifteen years and are discarded, of interest only to us historians who have little better to do than read through old documents and try to figure out what drove their authors to produce them.

The argument most often presented against the Rule of Saint Albert applying to the Carmelite Laity is that if they follow a Rule (that is in Latin, a *Regula*) the Laity become *Regulars*, that is Religious. This argument is not logical however. In the first place, the Carmelite Laity who followed the Rule of Saint Albert for four centuries before Theodore Straccio wrote the first Rule for the Third Order never became Religious. Even more to the point, if following a Rule makes the adherents Religious, than the current Third Order Rule makes them Religious. A Rule is a Rule. They should have no Rule at all if adherence to a Rule makes them Regulars! It could better be argued that Albert's Rule, which was written to be a *Formula Vitae*, a *Pattern for Life*, and which for the Laity could still be considered a *Pattern for Life*, is more appropriate to the lay status of the Third Order than any Rule, even a Rule written for the laity.

For several reasons then it is important that Lay Carmelites reappropriate for themselves the Rule of Saint Albert. It is the Rule of Saint Albert that makes us Carmelites. The Rule of Saint Albert is the common bond that unites the Carmelite family across the globe, in the different Orders and Congregations, and stretching back eight centuries. And it is the Rule of Saint Albert that provides a stability of vision that matures and develops with every generation of Carmelites but which never becomes obsolete. A careful look at the Rule of Saint Albert, or perhaps better, at Albert's *Pattern for Life*, will show how well suited it is for all Carmelites, Religious and Lay.

THE TEXT AND COMMENTARY
THE RULE OF SAINT ALBERT
REVISED BY POPE INNOCENT IV

CHAPTER 1

Albert, called by God's favour to be Patriarch of the Church of Jerusalem, bids health in the Lord and the blessing of the Holy Spirit to his beloved sons in Christ, B. and the other hermits under obedience to him, who live near the spring on Mount Carmel.

In this chapter, Albert addresses the Lay hermits. In doing so he clearly marks out the lines of distinction between his patriarchal authority and their status as subjects, but does so not without a certain affection It sets a hierarchical tone to the letter which today we may find a bit off-putting, but which was standard communication in Albert's day and which is still used in formal ecclesiastical documents. Albert is the Patriarch and his authority is by God's own favour. (Today, a bishop would add "by the favour of the Holy See," but in Albert's day bishops saw themselves in communion with the Holy See but not holding their authority from the Pope.) He is the Patriarch. The hermits are his sons. He has authority over them as a Father-in-Christ. Furthermore, he is Patriarch of Jerusalem–the most ancient and apostolic of sees, and the spiritual centre of the world. Jerusalem is the city that is the symbol of the heavenly city of the end time. The hermits, for their part, live near the spring on Mount Carmel, a sacred place to be sure, but not of the spiritual grandeur of Jerusalem. In this introduction Albert makes it very clear to everyone who holds the power. And yet, the letter has a tone of endearment. Albert, for all the grandeur of his position, loves the hermits as a father loves his sons and in this *Pattern for Life*, will look out for their good.

LAY CARMELITES AND THE RULE, CHAPTER 1

Well, we certainly start off in our proper place, whether we are Friars or Nuns or Laity. We are reminded where we stand in the hierarchical structure of the Church, and it is not near the top. Avery Dulles, S.J. in his wonderful book *Models of the Church*, a book that is over thirty years old but still worth reading, admits that the hierarchical and institutional model of the Church has been a bit overused these past centuries and declares that it is time to invest ourselves more in other models of Church–the Church as Servant, or the Church as Herald of the Gospel. Perhaps the most common model today is the Church as *communio*–a sacred bonding of members in the Body of Christ. Dulles' theology was validated when he was made a Cardinal in his senior years, but his point would still be well taken were he a simple priest teaching theology. Hierarchy and Institution hold little charm for us modern Christians and have even less credibility in the secular world. Nevertheless, as Dulles warns us, the Institutional/hierarchical model of the Church can be underplayed, but it cannot be done away with. The fact of the matter is that we stand in a hierarchical relationship with the rest of the Church.

In the concrete this means that we Carmelites, Religious and Lay, must remember the proper respect and obedience that is owed to those who stand above us in the Church. The Friars and many congregations of the Sisters have a different relationship with the bishop than do most of the Nuns and all the Laity. The bishop is often the major superior of a monastery of Nuns and has certain rights over them that he does not have over the friars or congregations of Sisters of Pontifical Jurisdiction. They are accountable directly to the Congregation of Religious in Rome. The Laity are invariably members of the local Church and as such have an obligation to show their bishops obedience and respect. (The Friars and Sisters also, in matters of the pastoral care of the bishop's faithful, must follow his directives. Their exemption applies only to those matters which are proper to the Order.)

This is important because sometimes Lay Carmelites have felt justified in disobeying their bishops and even in showing public displays of disrespect. Claiming that the bishop himself has been disobedient to the Holy See, they have felt justified in ignoring his policies and even demonstrating against him. Ultimately it is not our place to judge the fidelity of the bishop. If the Holy See wants to remove a bishop for disobedience or heresy, it is the responsibility of the Holy See to do so. In the meanwhile, we must show our bishops proper respect. We do not have to agree with the bishop, but our disagreement must always be with the proper respect and cannot be used to justify disobedience to him.

Carmelites need to cultivate good relations with their bishop. We are part of the Church and we exist to serve the Church in prayer and in cooperation with the apostolic mission. The Church never is helped by divisiveness and disharmony. This does not mean that we renounce our prophetic responsibility that is ours both by virtue of our baptismal anointing and our charism as the followers of the great prophet, Elijah, but it does mean that our prophetic voice must always be used to build up the Kingdom of God and not to tear apart the Church, the Body of Christ. A lack of charity is never permissible towards anyone, whatever their station. The truth, if it is God's truth, can be spoken with due respect for authority and profound love for all. If we do not build up the Body of Christ, then we should disband. Our vocation, Saint Thérèse said, is to be charity in the heart of the Church. We must work to build up the Body of Christ, cementing the different living stones from which God's earthly temple is constructed, with the love that comes to us from the Holy Spirit.

Chapter 2

Many and varied are the ways in which our saintly forefathers laid down how everyone, whatever his station or the kind of religious observance he has chosen, should live a life of allegiance to Jesus Christ – how, pure in heart and stout in conscience, he must be unswerving in the service of his Master.

Chapter 2, like chapter 1, is clearly a contribution of Albert and is a continuation of the previous chapter. However, Albert has moved from greeting the hermits to stating the purpose to which he wants the hermits to give themselves–a life of allegiance to Jesus Christ. Albert admits that there are many ways to do this. Albert was himself a Religious. He belonged to a community of Canons Regular known as the Canons Regular of the Holy Cross of Mortara. They had their own Rule, a Rule composed of the wisdom of many of the great Fathers of the Church–Saints Augustine, Jerome, Gregory the Great, Prosper of Aquitaine, and Isidore of Seville. It was called the Rule of the Holy Fathers. In addition he certainly was familiar with the monastic Rule of Benedict as well as the vast corpus of material written by John Cassian for his monks in the fifth century. When one looked at this vast body of spiritual literature, one realizes that there are indeed many ways in which one can live a life of discipleship of Jesus Christ. There are monks, anchorites, canons regular, and hermits of various types. In addition Albert was well aware that in the Church of his day new forms of Religious Life were emerging. And then there were the many devout men and women who did not want to become Religious at all, but who wanted to follow Christ in the lay life. These would include pilgrims, penitents, and various types of lay hermits, as well as *pinzocheri*–men and women who were leading devout lives in their own homes but under the guidance of some of the new Religious communities that were springing up. No matter what the form one chose, clerical or Religious or lay, living in the city or in the countryside, with vows or without, there was one thing in common to them all. They all wanted to live a life of allegiance to Jesus Christ.

Albert takes this idea of a life of allegiance to Jesus Christ and he makes it central to his project for the hermits. The term Albert uses is *vivere in obsequio Ihesu Christi*. It does not translate directly into English and "allegiance" is probably the best word for *obsequio* in this context that we can find. But in fact *obsequio* has rich layers of meaning that are lost in English. First of all it is related to the verb *sequi* which means to follow and it contains the idea of following Jesus. You may remember Jerome's famous phrase: *nudus nudum Christi sequi*–meaning to naked follow the naked Christ. It is a life of discipleship, and thus some like to translate it "in the footsteps of Jesus Christ," but this is only one layer of meaning and not the most important.

Craig Morrison says the phrase *in obsequio Ihesu Christi* is lifted from 2 Corinthians 10:5 and I think to appreciate Albert's reference it we need to establish its context in the two verses before as well.

"For although we are in the flesh, we do not battle according to the flesh, for the weapons of our battle are not of the flesh but are enormously powerful, capable of destroying fortresses. We destroy arguments and every pretension raising itself against the knowledge of God, and take every thought captive *in obedience to Christ*, and we are ready to punish every disobedience, once your obedience is complete."

The word *obsequio* can be rendered into English in several different ways. While we have chosen "allegiance" for Albert's use, the translators here choose the word obedience for the Latin *obsequio*, in Paul's writings, but that is not my point.[6] Notice that the idea of *obsequio*/ allegiance/ obedience appears in the context of battle–and spiritual battle, not an earthly battle. Moreover we are given weapons that are not of the flesh but are enormously powerful. Albert will pick up this idea again in chapters 18 and 19 when he talks about spiritual warfare and the armour of God with which we are to clothe ourselves. What is the connection then between *obsequio* and battle?

In the paper he delivered at Lisieux in 2005, Brother Patrick Mullins, O.Carm. explored the rich levels of meaning behind the word *obsequio*. In the Middle Ages,

---

[6] Remember too that Paul actually wrote in Greek, not Latin, so *obsequio* is not his word, but the way the translators of the New Testament into Latin chose to render the original Greek. This is the problem with translations that those who want the liturgical translations to be precise do not understand. Very few things translate directly from one language to another. No translation is more false than a literal translation. Every time something passes into a new language it looses something of the original and it picks up something of the new language that it originally did not have.

obsequio was the relationship which the knight pledged to his Lord. It is the idea of fealty. The knight becomes the liege Lord's man–vowed irrevocably to his service. He gives service to the Lord, fighting for him. And the Lord, in his part, is obligated to give protection and safety (*salus*) to the knight and his household and his possessions. It is a covenantal relationship in which *obsequio* (obedience, fealty, loyalty,) is exchanged for *salus* (safety, protection). But *salus* also means salvation! We who give our *obsequio* to Jesus Christ expect in return that he will offer us *salus*. We pledge our lives to fight for him, but our warfare is not earthly warfare. He pledges safety to us, but it is far more than any earthly safety! Albert is here setting the stage for the theme he will pick up again in chapters 18 and 19 of the Rule.

LAY CARMELITES AND THE RULE, CHAPTER 2

This chapter is remarkably important today when we find ourselves preoccupied with the idea of security. Terrorist bombings in New York, Washington, London, Madrid, Nairobi, Bali, not to mention the ongoing terrorism in Afghanistan, the Palestinian Territories, Israel, Lebanon, Iraq, Nigeria, the Philippines, Indonesia and other countries have given us a sense that there is precious little security available to any of us wherever we are in the world. The military response to terror has, if anything, made the situation worse and has planted seeds of terrorism in future generations. It is tempting to resort to violence to meet the violence, but in fact violence only sows the poisonous seeds of more and deeper violence.

There are voices of peace in our world. The Dalai Lama is a symbol of peace for many because of his profound teachings on the matter. Indeed Buddhism is a religion that rejects violence in any form. But all the great world religions, as well as the various local and tribal religions of the various indigenous peoples of the world, have voices that cry for peace. Religious leaders frequently gather in prayers for Peace. The late Pope John Paul II twice gathered religious leaders from around the world in Assisi to pray for peace. There are annual gatherings for prayers for peace by these same religious leaders sponsored by an Italian Catholic organization known as the Community of Sant'Egidio. Sincere people of every religion want peace.

Peace is not, of course, simply an absence of war. Peace requires that we construct a world in which war is not necessary. The nature of peace requires a foundation of justice. That is a very different type of world. There are many plans for peace. Over the years a succession of Secretaries-General of the United Nations, men like Dag Hammarskjöld and U Thant, have made appeals for peace. Archbishop Tutu, Martin Luther King, Mohandas Gandhi, John XXIII, and other world leaders have raised their voices for peace. As already mentioned, the Dalai Lama has been a tireless emissary of peace. Buddhist teacher Thich Nhat Hanh has spent his life travelling the world talking about peace. All these voices have made their contribution, but none have been able to bring peace.

There is one way to peace however which is yet to be tried. We have it in the Gospels. It sounds simplistic, but Christ has shown us a way to peace. It is a way that we, even we Christians, have rejected as impractical. O, we have tried in our various lives to put one part or another into practice, but too often we have concentrated more on the laws of the Church than on the Gospel of Christ. Mass on Sunday binds us, but forgiving our brother seventy-times seven is something we don't take seriously. We worry about meat on a fast day but we give little thought to loving our enemies and praying for our persecutors. Our spiritual lives too often have us straining gnats and swallowing camels. We Carmelites, Religious and Lay, in pledging our lives to living in allegiance to Jesus Christ, pledge to live the Gospel in its entirety and without compromise. That is not something that we do overnight. With each reading of the Gospel we see how much growth lies yet ahead of us. We never get there, but the important thing is that we stop compromising. We know the forgiveness begins with our own families and we humble ourselves to apologize and restore relationships in our families and among those who were once our friends even when the fault is not ours. We constantly examine ourselves to see where we can be more generous to those in need and gradually trim our lives of excess so that we can store up treasure in heaven. We give to Caesar what is Caesar's but we never yield to Caesar the demand that God has on our lives for obedience to his law. We remember that our true citizenship, our ultimate loyalty, is in heaven.

Of course, to live the Gospel we must know the Gospel and to know the Gospel we must read it. And we must pray it! Jesus speaks to us constantly. The

Carmelite lives out of the Word of God. It is our food and drink. No day goes by that we don't pick up the Gospel and nourish ourselves with Christ's saving word. All this will be more clear when we look at Chapter 19, the chapter on spiritual warfare and the armour of God.

CHAPTER 3

It is to me, however, that you have come for a Rule in keeping with your avowed purpose, a Rule you may hold fast to henceforward; and therefore:

This passage is obviously a transitional passage between Albert's introduction and the actual outline of life he has prepared for them. What is interesting, however, is that he mentions their "avowed purpose." In Latin this is *propositum vestrum* and it is best translated as "your proposal." In other words, when the hermits approached Albert for his blessing and asked him to lay out for them a way of life, they seem already to have had a plan in mind. Albert will modify that plan considerably, not so much changing it as adding to it and refining it. But it establishes a dialogical model between the hierarchical authority of the Church and the lived experience and experienced discernment of the hermits themselves. It is a dialogue that takes into account the higher authority of the Patriarch and yet which expects that the experience and vision of the hermits will be honoured in the final product. They are Albert's spiritual sons, but adult sons in an honest relationship with authority.

One point which needs to be clarified is that the translators here have chosen to translate the Latin *formula(m) vitae* as Rule and Rule of Life. Again, translations are never precise, but the Latin text does not speak of a *Regula(m),* that is a Rule, but of a document of lesser status, a *formula vitae* or "Pattern for Life." It only becomes a Rule in the proper sense when Innocent IV modifies it in 1247. A more literal translation of the Latin text would read:

"Truly, you have asked of us that we might, according to your proposal, grant you a pattern for life that you should henceforth keep."

This illustrates the problem we have with the liturgical translations. To translate literally provides awkward and clumsy texts and yet to provide a more smooth translation results in minor, but significant changes.

Lay Carmelites and the Rule, Chapter 3

This chapter again sheds light on our relationship to the larger Church. Just as the hermits approached Albert with respect, but with having thought out their ideas and discerned their vocation, we too are respectful and obedient to ecclesiastical authority, but in an adult fashion. We have a clear idea of our vocation as Carmelites, in our case today a vision that has eight centuries of history and is shared by the Carmelite family around the world. At the same time, we are responsive and flexible to the needs of the local Church. Our Carmelite vocation is never outside of our basic baptismal vocation to be healthy and constructive members of the Body of Christ, building up that Body in charity. We meet our bishop and our pastors with respect, but not with a childish subservience. We are not reluctant to express–in a respectful manner–our ideas, particularly regarding our vocation in the Church as Carmelites. We take direction from them as to how we can best serve the Church and yet we stay faithful to our vocation as Carmelites to be men and women of contemplation.

Sometimes bishops ask Carmelites to undertake a mission that is not proper to our vocation. Years ago, a Cardinal Archbishop in the United States asked the Discalced Carmelite Friars to open a High School in his Archdiocese. They declined because they understood that teaching is not a compatible ministry with the demands of the contemplative vocation as it is understood in the Discalced tradition. The Archbishop was angry and expelled them from his Archdiocese. It was a tremendous loss for them–emotionally and economically–but they had no choice if they were to be faithful to their vocation. Sometimes there is pressure on the cloistered Sisters to undertake a particular work, even a spiritual work, that would be disruptive of their contemplative life. We all understand that Carmel has a specific role in the Church and while we are flexible, we also must be faithful. Lay Carmelites too must be open to the needs of the Church but anxious to serve in those areas which are consistent with our vocation. There is much room for us to respond to the needs, but we also must keep our Carmelite focus. The Body of Christ has many members with diverse roles, we should not undertake the roles of other members of the Body. According to our individual talents we can do many things. We can teach religion; we can help with the care of the altar; we can serve on the finance board. As a community, however, we want to focus on bringing our tradition of prayer and spirituality to the larger Church. We want to gather people for prayer, help them learn about prayer. Organizing retreats and days of recollection can be a valuable contribution. Providing good reading material on spirituality is another way we can serve. But let the Third Order Dominicans run the local inquisition if they choose, that is not our task.[7]

---

[7] My apologies to any Dominicans who take umbrage with this role. I am certainly not encouraging anyone to undertake the personal responsibility for enforcing what they perceive to be orthodoxy "Truth" is the motto of the Dominican Order and the Dominicans have always been in the forefront of presenting the Truth of our faith, but as former Master General Timothy Radcliffe O.P. has written, Truth does not need to be defended. My point is that I am concerned to keep Carmelites out of a fray that we are ill-suited for. It is not our place to be the watchdogs of orthodoxy in the Church, it is our vocation to be Charity in the Heart of the Church.

Chapter 4

Albert
The first thing I require is for you to have a prior, one of yourselves, who is to be chosen for the office by common consent, or that of the greater and more mature part of you; each of the others must promise him obedience – of which, once promised, he must try to make his deeds the true reflection.

Pope Innocent IV (the 1247 revision)
The first thing I require is for you to have a prior, one of yourselves, who is to be chosen for the office by common consent, or that of the greater and more mature part of you; each of the others must promise him obedience – of which, once promised, he must try to make his deeds the true reflection – and also chastity and the renunciation of ownership.

Notice, first of all, that this is the first place where Pope Innocent IV and his advisors, Cardinal Hugh of Saint Cher and Bishop William of Tortosa, revised Albert's original *Pattern for Life*. This revision does not change the substance of Albert's text, but makes it conform to the Canon Law for Religious which requires the three vows of religion. The first thing Albert, and Innocent, tell the hermits is that they are to choose a prior and to promise him–and give him–obedience. There are several significant elements to this.

1. The leader of the community is a prior. He is not an abbot. Traditional monastic life was under the direc-

tion of an Abbot. The word abbot is derived from the word *abba*, father. An abbot governs his community as a father governs his family. In Benedictine and other monastic orders, the abbot was assisted by the senior brother of the community who was called the prior. By the eleventh century many Religious communities were doing away with the idea of an abbot because they saw themselves as a community of brothers and wished the leader of their community to be, not their father, but their older and wiser brother. In Carmel we do not have parental authority figures. Our prior is the first among equals, the first of the brothers or sisters of our family. And the leadership he or she exercises is not one of power, or even authority, but one which gathers the consensus of the whole family in decision making. At the time when the Carmelites were founded–and the Franciscans and Dominicans as well–the citizens of the towns were learning to govern themselves with democratic principles and democratic leadership models were borrowed by Religious communities. In Carmel decisions are made by the community not by the prior acting alone.

2. The prior is chosen by the community. He is not imposed from outside. Neither the king nor the bishop chooses the prior. Nor does the prior choose his successor. Ideally there is a consensus in choosing the prior, but when all cannot agree then wisdom is considered to dwell with the majority. Alas, that does not always prove true but if a community is mature and prayerful, its leadership will be sound.

3. The prior chosen is himself a member of the community. He does not come in from outside the membership. He has been part of the struggles and growth of the community. Now this has always been understood broadly–it is not necessary that the prior is a member of the particular Carmelite community which elects him, but rather that he is part of the Carmelite family. A Carmelite community may elect a prior from another Carmelite community. It simply means that we do not elect a Dominican or a Benedictine or a diocesan priest to be the prior. In the middle ages, superiors were sometimes appointed or elected from outside the Religious tradition of the community and this was almost always a disaster because the leader himself was not trained in the ways of the community he would lead. It is very important that leaders (and formation directors) be part of the community themselves and have grown up in the traditions of a particular community

4. The members of the community promise the prior their obedience. We owe our leadership our support and compliance. We have chosen them to lead and we must collaborate with them. The obedience is not to the person of the prior, but to the community which he represents and which has chosen him to lead. We can offer the prior obedience and respect because he offers us service, not domination. There is more to be said about this in chapters 22 and 23.

5. When Pope Innocent IV took Albert's *Pattern for Life* for lay hermits and converted it to a Rule for

Religious, he had to "bring it up to code," that is to say he had to make sure that it conformed to the canon law of the time for Religious. The canons decreed that Religious professed the three vows of Religion and so Innocent added to Albert's original formula the promises or vows of renunciation of ownership and chastity. Most lay hermit groups had only promised obedience–though all strove to imitate Christ in his chastity and in his poverty. Chastity and poverty were just understood to be essential to following Christ in the evangelical life. Chastity will surface later in the text in chapter 19, the renunciation of private property in chapter 12. Sometimes, however, it is best to take that which we understand to be a value and make it an explicit command.

LAY CARMELITES AND THE RULE, CHAPTER 4.

This chapter applies to Lay Carmelites on both the communal and personal levels.

On the communal level it tells us that leadership in Carmel is fraternal. The leader is not in any sense over or above the community. The leader is one of the community, one of the brothers or sisters of the family. Leadership is exercised in a fraternal and not a parental way. The leader does not make decisions for the community but listens to the brothers and sisters and helps the community grow in good decision-making. It tells us too that community chooses the leader. The parish priest or the spiritual assistant (chaplain) doesn't appoint the leader; even the bishop cannot appoint the leader.[8] It is also important to note that the parish priest has no governance of the internal decisions of the community though if the community is meeting in the parish he certainly has the right to decide when parish facilities are open to them and set policies for the use of the facilities for which he is responsible. Similarly the conduct of Lay Carmelites at parish liturgies and events must conform to his requests. They need to collaborate with him as far as they are able and should always try to be a positive influence in the parish. If they find themselves in conflict with the parish priest it is better that the community move to a new location than be in any way divisive in the parish.

It is also important to note that the outgoing leader or the community's council does not appoint the leader. The leader is chosen from the Lay Carmelites and by the community. It is permissible to choose a Lay Carmelite from another Lay Carmelite community, but this is exceptional. Normally someone from the community itself will be chosen.

On the personal level, Lay Carmelites must remember that following Christ in his poverty, his chastity, and his obedience is essential to our way of life. Of these three, the most important is obedience for obedi-

---

[8] When a community is being formed and until they have enough members to be a formed community, the provincial of the friars or his delegate, can appoint temporary leadership. And if a community finds itself in some difficulty, the provincial or his delegate can intervene as they would be able to intervene in a community of Friars or Nuns in the same situation.

ence to the will of the Father is Christ's most perfect virtue. It was by his obedience that he has saved us and saved all humankind. Obedience is always to be understood to be obedience to the Divine Will. This means that we seek conformity to the Word of God in our words and actions, and not just outward conformity but a deep conforming of our wills. It further means that we render due obedience to the Church through the Pope, our bishop, and the pastors of the Church. Incidentally, obedience to the Pope is given through obedience to the bishop.[9] Sometimes Lay Carmelites foment disobedience and disrespect toward a pastor or toward a bishop because they claim that the pastor or bishop is not loyal to papal authority. That is not for us to judge. The Pope can well defend his authority and does not need us to wage the local battles for him. If the Bishop is wrong or the pastor is wrong, let their superiors take care of the issue. Our vocation is to be charity in the heart of the Church, not a thorn in its side.

---

[9] Lay Carmelites must not disobey the bishop or be disruptive in the diocese alleging that they are being obedient to the Pope in doing so. Let the Pope decide if the bishop is being obedient, it is not for us to judge the bishop. The rights of bishops in their diocese to set norms, especially in matters liturgical, that differ from the universal law are too complex for most of us to figure out with certainty. It is up to the Holy See to enforce obedience, not us. While we always retain the right to question the Holy See about the bishop, or question the bishop about the local parish priest, in the meantime we should conform to the directives given us at the local level until we hear otherwise. Under no circumstances should we publicly challenge the authority of the bishop or the local pastor.

In regards to poverty, all Christians are called to live simply and with a mindfulness of the needs of those who lack necessities of life. The vow taken by the Religious is the vow of the renunciation of ownership which means that the individual Religious cedes all rights of ownership to the community. This is not practical for Lay Carmelites. But Lay Carmelites should keep the spirit of the vow both in trying to live ever more simply and in dedicating some portion of their material resources to the work of the Order. In terms of living more simply, as we mature in Christ and allow Christ to become our dearest possession, we simply find that we desire less and less of other things. For most of us, this is a long but determined process. Little things that once struck our fancy become seen for what they truly are–little things. As Christ becomes our all, Christ alone suffices. In terms of dedicating some portion of our goods to the mission of the Order, our love for Carmel makes us want to support its missionary activities, or its work among the poor at home, or the prayers of the cloistered Sisters. It becomes a joy for us to make small sacrifices that enable Carmel to spread. We stand in solidarity with the Carmelite family in real and true ways as our generosity educates young Carmelites, or provides medical supplies for Carmelite Sisters working in the missions, or provides some comfort for elderly Carmelites in a nursing facility. Jesus tells us that where our hearts are there too is our treasure. Our love for Carmel should motivate us to appropriate levels of financial support.

Chastity is a virtue for both the married and the single. For the married chastity means not only fidelity to one's spouse but a true appreciation of the sanctity of conjugal sex in the sacrament of marriage. In the Church we have often spoken too little about the sanctity of conjugal love. Married people, Carmelite or otherwise, are not called to celibacy. Certainly profession as a Lay Carmelite, holy as it is, does not take precedence of the Sacrament of Matrimony and the holiness proper to it. Celibacy within marriage is not a virtue, it is a rejection of an essential component of the sacrament of marriage. The sexual union of a husband and wife in generous self-giving of the each to the other is a sacramental mirror of the union of Christ and his Church in their unitive and ecstatic self-gift of each to the other. Of course there reasons in marriage, usually medical, when a couple must give up the use of lovemaking and then the same norms of celibate chastity apply. Married couples should avail themselves of good medical advice in trying to resolve these issues without losing their conjugal joys and duties to one another however. And both scripture and the tradition of the Church admit that husbands and wives might at times abstain from lovemaking to devote themselves–for a time–more intensely to prayer or some phase of the Lord's work. But such interruptions are not permanent vocational changes. The idea of people living celibately within marriage is most often rooted in a Jansenist view that human sexuality, even when expressed within the Sacrament of Matrimony, is–if not actually sinful–less holy than celibacy. But that is not the teaching of the Church. Nothing can be more holy than the self-surrender of the spouses to one another in physical union for this is, as I said before, the outward sign of the mystical union between Christ and his Church where we become one with the Lord of whose body we become members.

For those Lay Carmelites who are not married, the norms of celibate chastity apply of course, for we know that sex is too sacred for us to approach outside of the bonds of marriage. Because sex is the sacramental ground where the union of Christ and his Church is symbolized in the union of husband and wife, we who are without husband or wife keep our distance as a mark of the holiness of conjugal sex.

CHAPTER 5

Pope Innocent IV (the 1247 revision)
If the prior and brothers see fit, you may have foundations in solitary places, or where you are given a site that is suitable and convenient for the observance proper to your Order.

This chapter was not in Albert's *Pattern for Life* but was added when Pope Innocent IV adjusted Albert's text to become a Rule in 1247. The foundation on Mount Carmel was a place suitable for a certain amount of solitude, though this should not be over interpreted. We know that the fountain of Elijah which was at the entrance to their site was a popular spot for pilgrims to stop on their way down to Jerusalem. It would have marked a natural spot for their mid-day break on the first day of the pilgrimage, being about a five or six hour walk south of Acre, the starting point for most pilgrims on their journey to Jerusalem. And it would have been a perfect spot, of course, to water their animals and to find some refreshment themselves. Similarly, when Baron de

Grey established hermits from Mount Carmel at Aylesford, their hermitage was at a place where one of the principal pilgrim roads to Canterbury forded the river Medway and there seems to have been a pilgrim hostel at the place even before the Carmelites arrived there. It was not rare for hermits in the Middle Ages to care for pilgrims and offer them hospitality. Neither was it common, of course, for hermits, to establish themselves in busy towns or cities. Hermits traditionally lived outside the city or town walls, usually at some distance, where they could find quiet and a certain amount of solitude.

In his revision of Albert's text, Innocent gave permission for the Carmelites to accept sites in such solitary places or wherever they were given land that they judged suitable for their way of life. This was interpreted as permission to make foundations within the cities and towns, although not all Carmelites felt that such urban sites were appropriate to the observance proper to the Order. Nicholas Gallicus, the attributed author of *The Fiery Arrow*, was one voice that dissented from these new urban houses. Nevertheless, once Innocent added this paragraph, Carmelites have lived in towns and cities more often than not. The challenge is always to find within our busy lives the places of interior solitude and quiet that keep us faithful to our contemplative vocation.

LAY CARMELITES AND THE RULE, CHAPTER 5

Carmelites can live anywhere. We are flexible people. As we mature in the Lord's grace the externals of life matter less and less. It would be nice, some of us think, to live in the countryside. The quiet of rural life and the beauties of nature are great aids to the contemplative vocation, but we live where God calls us to live. Any place can be suitable. The challenge is not where we plant our feet–or our rump–but where we put our heart. Indeed, the city today is often the spiritual desert. The loneliness of the elderly trapped in their apartments, the plight of the inner-city poor, the fear of people who live behind locked doors, the insecurity of our streets–all this contributes to modern deserts that cry out for people to live there in prayer. The only salvation for the suffering of our world, including our urban poor and abandoned, is prayer and a contemplative presence in the midst of the suffering is a great sign of God's love. The suffering of the elderly, the poor, the broken family, the person trapped in addictions, all make good stuff for our prayer. We cannot become self-satisfied and complacent when surrounded by such human suffering. So city or village, town or country, apartment or farmhouse–we live in prayer wherever we are.

CHAPTER 6

Next, each one of you is to have a separate cell, situated as the lie of the land you propose to occupy may dictate, and allotted by disposition of the prior with the agreement of the other brothers, or the more mature among them.

In the Rule of Benedict monks are not given individual cells but live in a common dormitory. In the ancient monastic communities of Egypt and the near east, a senior monk often shared his cell with a novice or with several younger monks for whose training the senior was responsible, though that cell might often be a multi-room dwelling. Even among hermits, each one having his own cell was not a universal practice. Indeed among the lay hermits whom Francis of Assisi gathered together into his fledgling community their commitment to poverty made them share a common dormitory at San Damiano or at the Rivo Torto when the luxury of individual cells was not at hand. But when one reads Albert's original Latin text, the hermits of Carmel were told that each was to have not only his own individual cell, but a cell that was actually *separated* from the others–that is a separate location–whether it be a hut or a cave.

Probably most of the hermits on Carmel lived in small huts constructed of branches and mud. While there are a few caves at the site of the original foundation, they are only a few and even these are not suitable for habitation. But the climate is mild enough that a wattle hut would serve a hermit very well. Albert did not prescribe any arrangement for the colony–other than locating the chapel in the centre of the cells and the prior's cell at the entrance to the place. As to everything else–he simply directed that they should use their judgement according to the terrain. The wadi 'ain es-Siah is not a particularly large place, but certainly was adequate for the hermits to have their cells and whatever small garden each might cultivate. The hermits were reminded, however, that the cells were not theirs but allotted to them by the community. They were not free to trade cells among themselves but always were required to consult the prior and the other brothers about their living arrangements. While their life-style allowed each a tremendous amount of privacy and demanded that each take a large share of personal responsibility, ultimately they were to remember they were part of a community and not individuals.

LAY CARMELITES AND THE RULE, CHAPTER 6

A separate room, much less a separate little house, is a luxury beyond what most Lay Carmelites find in their lives. Indeed, the marriage vocation of the majority of our lay members usually requires that they not have a separate room–at least for sleeping. But sometimes it is possible to fix up a little place in our home to which we can retreat to read and study and pray. After the children "leave the nest" there might be room. Or a spare bedroom can become a little place to which we can withdraw when there are no guests visiting. Sometimes it might be just a corner of our room where we can put a chair and a table for our bible and perhaps a crucifix or an icon. Johanna Wesley, the mother of the famous founders of the Methodist movement, was a devout Anglican housewife, married to a parson and with nineteen children (ten of whom survived to adulthood). She would sit by the fire in her kitchen and put her apron up over her head and her children knew that when their mother was in her "prayer tent" she was not to be disturbed. Her example of frequent prayer bore great fruit in her sons John and Charles who themselves became two pillars of Protestant Spiritual Literature and whose influence has spilled over, especially through their wonderful hymns, into our Catholic Church. (Incidentally, John Wesley was a great reader and admirer of the Discalced Carmelite mystic, Brother Lawrence of the Resurrection.) Solitude can be found anywhere. Blessed Titus Brandsma wrote that the six weeks he spent at Scheveningen prison were the most peaceful and contemplative part of his life, despite his confinement in a small cell open to the vision of all in the prison. He wrote of it:

"Blessed Solitude. I already feel completely at home in this little cell. I haven't been bored at all, in fact just the opposite. I am here alone, but never was our Lord so close to me. I could shout for joy that He has again let himself be found by me without me being able to be among people or people with me. He is now my only refuge and I feel safe and happy. I would like to stay here always, if He wills that. I have seldom been so happy and so content."

The Buddhist monastic tradition says that a monk can find his cell in a tavern, while a reprobate will find a tavern in his cell. The cell is ultimately a state of mind, an ability to retreat to an inner place in the heart where, whatever our external condition is, we can find the solitude in which Christ is our only companion, the only focus of our attention. But this requires practice, constant practice. We must avail ourselves of whatever solitude we do find–time alone in the car, time in the morning before the household comes to life, time that we wake in the middle of the night, a few stolen minutes in a church–we must use whatever solitude we do find to cultivate the practice of the inner cell, the cell of the heart. Once we learn the way there we can return there under almost any circumstances. Of course we must remember that charity for the needs of another must always draw us out. Christ will not be truly present to us in solitude unless we can be fully present to him in the needs of our neighbour.

Chapter 7

Pope Innocent IV (the 1247 revision)
However, you are to eat whatever may have been given you in a common refectory, listening together meanwhile to a reading from Holy Scripture where that can be done without difficulty.

This chapter too was added by Innocent's revisors in 1247. Originally the hermits ate their meals alone in their cells. They received what they needed from the brother appointed by the prior to see to the needs of the others, but they did not leave their cells for meals. This was actually unusual, even for hermits, because eating together was seen to be an essential part of the evangelical life. Most other groups wanted their members to imitate Christ and the apostles in breaking bread together. Even the strict monastic hermits like the Carthusians ate together at least weekly.

Common meals created some problems. It is more convenient to eat at our own schedule. We do not all like to eat at the same times of day. Also, at a common table we are more or less bound to the same food and that does not always suit us either. This is not just a matter of likes and dislikes, but, in fact, each of us has somewhat unique needs. But Innocent saw the common table as being very important. It was a time for the community to be nourished together, not only with earthly food, but with the Word of God which was to be read to them during the meal time. After Innocent's revisions, the Carmelites did not talk freely during their meals. Meals were not a time of socialization, but of prayer. The scripture was read to them as they ate so that they would remember that we do not live by bread alone but by every Word that comes from the mouth of God. Furthermore, it is good discipline to eat not when and what we want, but at the convenience of others. It is always good to have to live to the convenience of others, it helps us overcome our tendencies to self-centeredness.

Today most Carmelite Religious speak during the meals. It is common practice to begin the meal with a short scripture reading after the table prayers. Sometimes one of the readings from the Mass of the day is read. Ideally this set the tone for the conversation at the mealtime. But mealtime is often the only time we have as a family to talk with one another. Meals are an important recreational time.

LAY CARMELITES AND THE RULE, CHAPTER 7.

It is important that our Lay Carmelite meetings include some social time including time to share some food and drink. We may not always have an actual meal together, but the sharing of food and drink is an important part of human bonding for any family or any community. Our meal time, or our time with coffee and cake, is an ideal time for our *lectio divina*. It can help set a relaxed and conversational tone to our sharing how the Word of God speaks to us.

In addition to our meetings, we should have time together as a community to socialize together. English speakers are often more businesslike and make clear distinctions between those with whom we associate for work or projects and those with whom we have a friendship or familial relationship. Americans (and I am an American saying this) are particularly prone not to want to socialize with those with whom we associate professionally or through organizations. But we must remember that Carmel is not an organization, it is a spiritual family and we must be open to friendship and caring among our communities. We need to socialize with one another, both as a community and as individuals, beyond our formal times together. Food and drink–combined with prayer–enriches our time in each other's company.

Just as a note to this, I remember some years back being invited by a priest who is a member of a very traditionalist community to stop by and drop off a Christmas present his father had asked me to bring him while I traveled through the city where he lived. (The son lived in Europe, the father in the States.) I say that the community to which the son belonged was traditionalist, not traditional–there is a difference which I will explain in a moment. It was a cold and wet wintry day, just after Christmas. I walked from our monastery to his house, about forty-five minutes away. When I arrived I was shown into a parlor and the priest presently came and introduced himself. We had a very pleasant visit. I stayed over an hour. He showed me the chapel and the tomb of their founder who had been recently canonized. Their house was lovely, elegantly furnished. The chapel was magnificent with good quality stained glass and marble. In fact, everything was perfect. But I was never offered so much as a glass of water. This was Christmas week. There would have been no fast or any other reason not to offer hospitality. I don't believe it was the priest. He was gentlemanly in every other respect. A lapse of courtesy would be unusual on his part, I knew his parents, and how he was raised. I can only conclude that it was the policy of the community that refreshments were not offered to guests. This is one of the reasons I say the community was traditionalist, not traditional. Nothing is more traditional than offering hospitality. In any society, the first thing we offer guests is food, or at least drink. In monastic communities it is almost embarrassing how fast–and how much–refreshment is offered to guests. When people come to our homes and to our communities, refreshment should always be part of our hospitality. It does not have to be elaborate. A cup of tea is sufficient. But all guests should be received as Christ. Don't underestimate the importance of food and drink. Christ thought enough of it to make it the means of his abiding presence in the Church in the Sacrament of the Eucharist.

Chapter 8

None of the brothers is to occupy a cell other than that allotted to him or to exchange cells with another, without leave or whoever is prior at the time.

This chapter reminded the hermits that even their cell was not their own. They could not exchange it with another for a cell they preferred. The property belonged to the community, not to the individual. It also addressed the problem of the individual who thinks he could pray better if he were somewhere else. This is a common problem in the spiritual life–we look to external reasons to see why we don't advance instead of looking into the need for further purification of the heart and its attachments. We think "if I had a better view...," or "if I weren't so cold in this cell....then my heart would be lifted to God and I could concentrate on my prayers." Albert, or whoever drafted this chapter, knew that externals were never the issue. The cell that matters is the cell of the heart, the cell that is beyond any and all attachment to externals.

Lay Carmelites and the Rule, Chapter 8

We too must learn to bloom where we are planted. We fuss about the externals of our spiritual life and fail to deepen interiorly. "If only there was a statute in this chapel, then I could pray." "If only they had organ music rather than guitars, then I could concentrate on the Mass." "I can't concentrate on my prayers until everything is put away." "This house is too noisy for me to pray." As we mature spiritually we need less and less attention to the externals of our situation. As we mature spiritually we realize that life and every thing in it is a gift from God and not a distraction. We learn how to take the very things that annoy or distract us and make them useful in our spiritual life. The sound of children playing in the yard, even when they are loud and boisterous, becomes something that moves our hearts to gratitude rather than annoyance. We learn to welcome Christ into our house amid the clutter of undone dishes and yesterday's newspapers. In fact, we learn that Christ loves a messy house and is right at home there. He wants our attention for himself, not the house to have it. While we might appreciate the externals–a candle, devotional music, an icon–we need them less and less. We learn to put ourselves in the silent presence of God wherever we are–in the hammock in the yard, in an airplane, waiting in line at the supermarket. When life offers us the chance for silence and solitude–on a retreat, when no one else is home, before morning Mass in the church–we are grateful. And when life crowds in with noise and busyness, we learn to pay attention to the task at hand, and if possible without ignoring that task, to retreat to the silent and solitary place in our own heart.

We also need to remember that the treasures life offers us, including our homes, are not ours except to use. They once belonged to someone else and they will belong to someone else again. If we have been blessed with a beautiful home we should be deeply grateful, and anxious to relieve the sufferings of those who have no home. We are only stewards and God has entrusted us with what we have to use what he has given us to build up his kingdom. We should make our homes as nice as we can, not for our sake, but for the sake of our family and so that we can welcome guests and make them feel appreciated. We would welcome all guests as we would welcome Christ. And we must always be willing to put away our personal time with Christ in prayer to attend to Christ who knocks at our door. Remember, he does not always come in the guise of the poor, but he also comes as neighbour, relative, and friend. Our home is open to Christ because it must be open to all, and our home is open to all because we remember it is not ours but God's and he has given it to us for his will to be done.

CHAPTER 9

The prior's cell should stand near the entrance to your property, so that he may be the first to meet those who approach, and whatever has to be done in consequence may all be carried out as he may decide and order.

This is a practical matter that Albert and the hermits arranged. In ancient desert monastic settlements the cell of the *abba* was at the entrance to the site not only so that he could regulate the coming and going of the monks, but so that he could interview prospective candidates before they were allowed into the community. It was an eminently practicable decision and it is followed here as well. The prior will deal with the everyday decisions that tie the community to the world beyond the hermitage so that not everyone has to become involved in all the routine business of life. The prior also has the responsibility to welcome guests precisely to free the other hermits from constant distraction. The site of their hermitage was along a busy pilgrim route. Apparently many people stopped by to refresh themselves and their animals on the way down to Jerusalem. The hermits even went to the Holy See to get indulgences attached to those who stopped and visited their small oratory–in part because the alms of these pilgrims helped support the hermits. Yet all this coming and going would have made the contemplative life a difficulty for those in the hermitages. Someone had to tend to the pilgrims and look after their needs as well as to regulate their entry into the oratory and insure that they left the colony without disturbing the hermits. So the prior surrendered his solitude and silence to protect that of the others. The prior, of course, would have been one of the more spiritually mature hermits, one who knew how to keep his contemplative heart focused even in the midst of conversations and guests and all the comings and goings. It was a valuable service to render to the brothers and most priors were probably happy when their time of service was over and they could retire to the silence and solitude of a less busy cell.

LAY CARMELITES AND THE RULE, CHAPTER 9.

This chapter is about some very practical things. It is not particularly deep or inspiring, but attends to the mundane matters of every day life. Even on the spiritual heights of Carmel, after all, most of our life is about the mundane. The Lay Carmelite can take several lessons from it. First of all, hospitality is a virtue to which we must always attend. We cannot leave Christ standing unwelcomed in his physical presence because we are supposedly searching for him in some spiritual presence in our hearts. Christianity is full of stories of Christ coming to peoples' doors in the guise of a beggar, or an old person, or a child. The wise welcome him, often unseeing until afterwards, but wise enough, none the less, to put down their prayerbook and offer the guest some attention. The Incarnation is the central mystery of our Christian faith, and when we understand that we realize that the Incarnation is not limited to the unique manifestation of God in Jesus of Nazareth but that that God takes flesh in every human person. It amazes me that people claim to recognize Christ in bread and wine, and ignore him in flesh and blood. So hospitality must always be a virtue among us.

It also tells us in our Lay Carmelite vocation not to get involved in every issue and decision that comes along. We have leaders in our communities–priors, presidents, directors–precisely so they can worry, with the advice of their councils of course, about the every day decisions and leave the rest of us free for prayer, community, and ministry. We don't have to second guess every decision of the council. We should concentrate on the task at hand.

I remember one time doing a workshop in a monastery of Carmelite Nuns. The week that I was teaching, they were also in the process of buying a new car. The prioress and the treasurer had worked out the finances and the best model for what they could afford, but for some reason they brought the decision about the colour of the car and its upholstery to the community for a decision. It would have been comical if it were not a pathetic waste of time. Fifteen women trying come to a consensus on the colour of a car is not a pretty sight. If this sounds sexist, let me admit that men would have the same problems–probably not in the colour of a car–with choosing a widescreen television. We don't have to be part of every decision. There are decisions that are important to involve the whole community, and there are decisions that we should be willing to allow others to make and not busy ourselves with inconsequential matters. We need to let go of ninety percent of the things that matter to us. We need to invest our energy in the things that matter–in the love of God in prayer and the love of our neighbour in service.

Chapter 10

Each one of you is to stay in his own cell or nearby, pondering the Lord's law day and night and keeping watch at his prayers unless attending to some other duty.

This chapter has often been considered to be the "heart" of the Rule, although as I have pointed out, I believe that if there is any one section which is pivotal to the Rule of Saint Albert it is the section on Spiritual Warfare and the Armour of God because of the link between his *exordium* (to live a life of allegiance to Jesus Christ) and the idea of how we are to serve him faithfully, waging the spiritual warfare with the Armour of God, and receiving his corresponding promise of salvation. Nevertheless, this chapter is certainly one of the most crucial ones in the Rule. It may in fact be from Albert and, even if the idea for it was in the hermits' proposal to the patriarch, Albert certainly rewrote it as the use of scripture in it clearly bears his signature. Albert very artfully pasted together the phrase from Psalm 1:2 "pondering the Lord's law day and night" with an allusion to 1 Peter 4:7, telling the hermit to keep watch at his prayers. Morrison points out that the reference to 1 Peter actually uses an image that can be found several places in the New Testament where the disciples are encouraged to keep watch at prayer– Matt 26:41; Mark 13:33; 14:38; and Luke 21:36 as well as the Pauline exhortations to vigilance in prayer to be found in Colossians 4:2 and Ephesians 6:18. In other words, this is a very rich passage in its scriptural foundations and moreover one in which the juxtaposition of the texts opens up to the reader levels of meaning in the texts that one might otherwise overlook. It is as if each text helps us understand the others. This is a signature technique of Albert in his use of scripture. Keeping watch at our prayers reinforces and interprets the idea of meditation day and night on the Law of the Lord, and meditating day and night on the Law of the Lord tells us how to keep watch at our prayers. If it was part of the hermits' original proposal that they submitted to Albert, he considered it important enough to the project to embroider it with his scriptural rewriting–something that was not done for most of the surrounding chapters of the Rule which are quite plain and left bereft of any scriptural language.

Lay Carmelites and the Rule, Chapter 10.

We certainly want to take this chapter to heart. We might think that it is highly impractical for us to remain so stationery, never leaving our home, so that we can devote ourselves to constant prayer, but that is not what this chapter means. In the first place, the cell is the cell of the heart. We must learn how to remain in the cell of our heart, that is, to remain spiritually centred throughout our day. Saint Teresa, in the *Interior Castle*, speaks of the innermost dwelling place of the seventh and final mansion, which is the most secret chamber of our heart and which is large enough only for Christ and ourselves to enter. We must find that secret dwelling place where Christ is always present, waiting for us. As Teresa points out in the *Interior Castle*, we do not come quickly or easily to that cell. It is a long process of the spiritual life by which we discover the way. Part of that process requires us to have physical solitude where we can learn how to find, and be comfortable in, the psychological solitude in which this cell of the heart is located. In other words, as we grow in the spiritual life we need times and places, and prolonged periods of time, where we can learn to cherish a solitude that admits no loneliness. We need, Teresa tells us, to face honestly the terrors of being alone and coming to know ourselves for who we truly are. The stories of the ancient desert monks and nuns often speak of their encounters with lions or snakes or dragons. These stories are not to be taken literally. The beasts we face in solitude are the reflections we see of our sinful selves. In solitude we come to honestly wrestle with our pride, our avarice, our concupiscence, and all our failings, sins, and faults of whatever sort. We are faced with the challenge of self-knowledge and in coming to know ourselves we learn and own many things about ourselves which are not flattering. But we also learn to submit our brokenness and even our sinfulness to the light of Christ's mercy which not only forgives our past but slowly heals the wounds that have disfigured us and made us the sin-pocked folk we are. Only when we face honestly into our sin can we be healed of it and grow beyond it. That is why the Publican in the Gospel went home justified and the Pharisee, who counted only his righteousness, did not. But this long path through the soul that brings us to the solitary chamber where Christ awaits us is not only about confronting our sinfulness, it is also about experiencing the mercy of God who calls us into silent and wordless communion with him. We learn to sit silently in prayer, to move beyond words and deep into a consciousness of being that we had not previously known. We find ourselves coming into a profound and wordless communion with Being Itself, a communion that gives us a peace that is beyond our power to imagine until we have tasted it for ourselves. And in this peace, little by little we find our wilfulness surrendering itself, desiring only God. As we grow in this grace more and more we want nothing, nothing at all. All that once attracted us means little to us. The only thing that matters is God himself and we realize that to possess God we must be free of the desire to possess any other thing. We are sure of nothing, not even sure of our own existence, but only of God. This is not a path of continuous and unbroken progress. We go forward on it and then we go back again. At times we find ourselves beyond all the faults that once controlled us, and at times we find ourselves slipping back down the slope into wanting things our own way and at our own time. We find that at times we want only God, and at times we crave all sorts of things, good things, but things that distract us from the ultimate good which is only God. There are times when God seems so very close, and there are times when he seems so far away. There are times of great peace and there are times when we are utterly devoid of feeling, impatient at prayer, angry and frustrated because we can't seem to make any progress, indeed not wanting to make any progress but only getting our selfish life back and reclaiming on our own self-centred agenda. But then we realize that if we were to walk away from the journey, we would be more unhappy yet. Once we have come this far, we can't go back again. For awhile we may be happy in neither state. The things of God only frustrate us, the things of our old life, even the good things, leave us empty and unsatisfied. If we persist in prayer, however, the progress is made, however slowly. We no longer look for delight, even spiritual delight. We simply take what God gives us and journey on. Strangely, this journey is not just spiritual. In fact, as we progress in prayer our path takes us even more closely to the world, not farther away from it. But we see the world in a new light. We see suffering and we see sin and our heart breaks because it is more than we can address. We see that we can't fix our world, we can't fix our lives, we can't make any difference, but we realize that we can stop thinking of ourselves and we can start seeing the world in the way that God sees it. We stop judging others and learn compassion for them. We find that nothing scandalizes us anymore. We see human weakness, even sin, and we are moved only by understanding, pity, compassion, and love. We see people whose lives are a mess and we recognize ourselves in them and all we can feel is the compassion for them that God has felt for us. We see the world for what it lacks, we see the lovelessness of so many who are trapped in loneliness and pain and despair. We ourselves grieve that we do not have more love to give to heal the pain and brokenness we see. And at the same time that we realize how powerless we are to fix any of this brokenness, we find two great gifts within us. We find a tremendous confidence that prayer has a power that even our best actions do not. And we find that love, the love that energizes our prayer, has a great power. We find in ourselves great depths of patience, of understanding, of generosity–not just as feelings, but in empowering us to act in ways we have not been able to act before. We find that we have great power to be kind to those whom we once looked down on, disliked, or even hated. We still may not like them, but our feelings toward them are not relevant, our actions are not driven by our feelings. Indeed, we scarcely notice our feelings, much less find ourselves governed by them. This is not our doing, of course, it is all grace. We are slowly being transformed into the One Whom we love. We find ourselves becoming one with God and one with his creation. We become a bridge between heaven and earth and consequently our prayer on behalf of others becomes very powerful for in our heart is united the one for whom we pray and the One to Whom we pray. This is the path to the inner cell that Teresa talks about in the *Interior Castle*. But we must always be willing to leave that cell when the demands of charity call. Teresa, in one of the most beautiful passages she has written says:

"O my Jesus, how great is the love You bear the children of men, for the greatest service one can render You is to leave You for their sake and their benefit–and then You are possessed more completely. ... Whoever fails to love his neighbour, fails to love You, my Lord, since we see You showed the very great love You have for the children of Adam by shedding so much blood".[10]

Another way at which we can look at this cell of the heart, this psychological state, that calls us to constant

---

[10] Teresa of Jesus, *Soliloquies*, II 2

meditation on the Word of God is through the perspective of Saint Thérèse of the Child Jesus who confided that she never went for more than three minutes without thinking of her Lord. Thérèse was a busy woman in her monastery. She served in a number of key posts–assistant novice director (in fact, she was the acting novice mistress), and sacristan among others. As one of the younger nuns she had more than her share of the household duties. She was not able to remain physically in her cell. But she too knew that the cell is ultimately a place of the heart. We need physical–and psychological–solitude to learn to find this hidden chamber of the heart but once we know the way we can retreat to it at any time, though again always ready to come out for the sake of charity for anyone who needs us. We can turn our attention to the Lord while we are busy about the tasks of the day or when we are in crowded company. The Lord–and his word–is always a refuge for us in the business of life. We have already seen the wisdom of the Buddhist mystics who put it well: a monk can find a cell in a tavern and a ne'er-do-well can make a tavern out of a cell.

The lie we must never fall into is that we should not leave our cell when the needs of another call. Albert tells the hermits they are to leave their cell to attend to their other duties and we too must always be willing to leave when our neighbour is in need. The irony is that while the inner cell is only big enough to hold Christ and ourselves it cannot shut the world out. If we do not leave Christ to go to our neighbour in need, Christ will leave us. If our heart is too narrow for others, it will be too narrow for Christ. The surest measure of our love of Christ, in fact the only infallible measure of our spiritual growth, is the love we bear for others. Visions, locutions, spiritual insight, gifts of healing–all these can be counterfeited. The one infallible proof of grace is charity. The Evil One will never counterfeit charity–it undermines his campaign to destroy us and gives God the victory. And the narcissistic and self-deceiving ego, the usual source of counterfeit spirituality, is too self-involved to think of counterfeiting charity. Charity is always from God.

Saying that, of course, it is important to note that charity should not be confused with being nice. Being loving is seeking the good of the other. It usually involves being nice, but at times the good of the other requires a certain frankness on our part that most often will not be perceived as niceness. Charity is truthful, usually gently so, but sometimes bluntly. Charity at times demands confrontation. Niceness is usually called for but it can also be a means of avoiding the real needs of the other. It is a delicate balance. Jesus himself at times was blunt, even confronting. We think of him lovingly but there were certainly people in his own day who did not see him that way at all. And when others are blunt with us, or confronting, and seem to us to be harsh, we should listen carefully to what they have to say and weigh their words prayerfully. If need be we should ask one or two others, and not necessarily our good friends, what they think of the matter. Would that the Pharisees had weighed the words of Jesus to them! He spoke to them in love. Just because someone speaks harshly to us does not mean that their words are not profoundly charitable words.

This is all matter we should take to that inner cell and reflect on, pondering the Lord's law day and night, and keeping vigil at our prayers. On the other hand remember that some people, even some scapular-wearing church-goers, just are nasty. Have compassion for them, but don't take nasty people seriously. Life is too short to let ourselves be victimized by other people's spite. God did not create us to take grief.

CHAPTER 11

Albert
Those who know their letters and how to read the psalms, should, for each of the hours, say those our holy predecessors laid down and the approved custom of the Church appoints for that hour. Those who do not know their letters must say twenty-five 'Our Fathers" for the night office, except on Sundays and solemnities when the number is to be doubled so that the 'Our Father' is said fifty times; the same prayer must be said seven times in the morning in place of Lauds and seven times too for each of the other hours, except for Vespers when it must be said fifteen times.

Pope Innocent IV (the 1247 revision)
Those who know how to say the canonical hours with those in orders should do so, in the way those holy forefathers of ours laid down, and according to the Church's approved custom. Those who do not know the hours must say twenty-five Our Fathers for

the night office, except on Sundays and solemnities when that number is to be doubled so that the Our Father is said fifty times; the same prayer must be said seven times in the morning in place of Lauds, and seven times too for each of the other hours, except for Vespers when it must be said fifteen times.

When Albert first wrote his *Pattern for Life* for the hermits on Mount Carmel he devised a very interesting form of prayer to occupy their day. Some groups of lay hermits recited the Divine Office together as did clergy and Religious. These groups most likely would have had some number of clergy among their number who would have had to say the Divine Office in any case and so the Divine Office became the pattern for their community prayer. Other lay hermit communities emphasized individual prayer through the day. Some groups would have their members recite a prayer of aspiration such as "My Jesus Mercy on me a sinner" multiple times–hundreds of times perhaps–and sometimes each recitation combined with a genuflection or prostration. Others might recite specific psalms–perhaps the penitential psalms or the gradual psalms. Albert required the Latin hermits on Mount Carmel to recite the psalms appropriate to the Divine Office. This is curious because while he did not require the whole Office to be said, he was, in effect, imposing part of it on the lay hermits. Perhaps some of the lay hermits were clerics and familiar with the Office. Certainly someone had to inform the hermits who could read but who were not clerics which psalms they were to recite. It is a curious custom and I suspect that even early on Albert may have foreseen the day coming–which it did in only a few decades–when enough of the hermits might be clerics that the Divine Office itself would be the normative prayer. This requirement of the psalms of the Office seems as if it may have been a sort of intermediate step towards the common Office.

When Albert wrote that this obligation applied to those hermits who knew their letters and could read, he meant that those who knew Latin were to say the psalms. The Psalter would have been prayed in Latin and at least a rudimentary knowledge of that language would be required, as well as the ability to actually read, for the hermits to pray the psalms as Albert wished. This does not necessarily mean that each of the hermits had a Psalter, much less a breviary or a bible. They may well have been expected to know the Psalter, in Latin, by heart. That sounds like a lot of memorization to us moderns, but would not have been unusual in the Middle Ages. The constant repetition of the psalms–in the Divine Office each psalm was said at least once a week and many psalms were said much more often–would have had the hermits knowing the psalms by heart quite quickly. Psalms were often sung or chanted, the music being a pneumonic device that assisted the memory to recapture the words. The desert monks in the early centuries had been required to know the Psalter by heart and the medieval canon law required bishops to know the Psalter, though that was probably honoured more in the breach than in the observance when we see the level of spirituality of many medieval prelates. Before the invention of the printing press and the widespread distribution of books, a culture of memorization prevailed where people were far more disciplined than are we moderns for committing things to memory.

As early as 1229 there was a papal bull to the hermits that referred to them celebrating the Divine Office in their oratory. Another bull issued four days earlier mentioned the hermits leaving the colony on Mount Carmel to seek ordination and then returning to the hermitage. This indicates that within that first generation after Albert the community was clericalizing. One of the effects of clericalization was that the hermits were now obligated to recite not merely the Psalter as individuals, but the Divine Office itself which was normally recited in common and publicly in the community's chapel or church. When Innocent IV revised the Rule in 1247 he took this into account. In the bull *Paganorum Incursus*, issued several years earlier, he had made reference to the Carmelites celebrating the Divine Office in their churches. In revising the Rule he replaced Albert's instruction about praying the psalms appointed for the Office in their cells with the requirement of praying the Office itself in common.

Thus from early in their history, the Carmelites, like the other mendicant Orders, celebrated the Liturgy of the Hours in common and with a certain liturgical style, but they never embraced the long and florid Offices of the monastic Orders. In the Benedictine tradition, the Liturgy is its own end and its celebration is meant to be the summit of the monastic prayer. In the Carmelite tradition, the Liturgy prepares and nourish-es us for our contemplative prayer which is carried out in the secrecy of our cell. The monk contemplates while he sings the Office. The Carmelite may find himself, or herself, moved to contemplation in the Office, but is always anxious to return to the solitude where that contemplation is most comfortable.

There was always the question of those who were not literate and who did not know Latin. Albert provided a very simple Office of Our Fathers for them. This was a standard practice both for lay hermits and for the lay brothers in monastic communities. A similar Hail Mary Office said in place of the Little Office of the Blessed Virgin Mary by many laity evolved into our practice of the Rosary.

Lay Carmelites and the Rule, Chapter 11.

Before the Council it was the practice for the Third Order, as well as for many others in the Church, to pray the Little Office of the Blessed Virgin Mary. The Divine Office was available only in Latin and so was beyond the ability of many lay people–or even the Religious Brothers and Sisters of the Order–to pray. One of the first changes mandated by Vatican II was to allow the translation of the Divine Office, now usually referred to by its more ancient title of "The Hours" or "The Liturgy of the Hours" to be prayed in the vernacular. Once the Liturgy of the Hours became available in the vernacular it took precedence over all other forms of prayer other than the Mass itself. That is because, like the Mass and the administration of the

Sacraments, the Liturgy of the Hours is the official liturgy of the Church while various other prayers, including the rosary and approved litanies, are merely devotional prayers. The Church is anxious to see the Liturgy of the Hours become what it is meant to be–the Prayer of the Church–and so the laity are encouraged to pray it. Our Lay Carmelites are encouraged also to pray it, uniting themselves in prayer to the rest of the Carmelite family and to the larger Church. It should be the normal prayer when the community gathers. In some places, the Lay Carmelites gather with their parish family in the church to pray Morning or Evening Prayer. When we gather for the funeral vigil of one of our members, it should be our prayer as we pray the "Office of the Dead."

Lay Carmelites find that the bulk of their prayer-life is by themselves. Even for the Religious, far more time is normally spent in meditation, spiritual reading, and private prayer than in the communal Liturgy of the Hours and Mass. We have an eremitical spirituality and cherish solitary prayer. Of course no prayer is really solitary as in all prayer, even prayer alone, we are spiritually united with Christ and through Christ to the rest of the praying Church. Nevertheless, while Religious gather together through the day (and sometimes in the night) to pray the Liturgy of the Hours, most Lay Carmelites would usually say this prayer alone. It is prayed differently alone than in common.

When we pray the Liturgy of the Hours by ourselves there is no need to keep a common pace. We can take whatever time we have. If a psalm strikes us in a particular way, we can stay with that psalm for awhile. We may want to read it a second or a third time. A psalm or a reading may open the door of mental prayer to us, suggesting something deep within our heart. In private recitation we can pursue that. We can even close our breviary and use the remainder of our time to listen quietly to the Lord as his Word speaks to our innermost self. There is nothing magical about saying all the words or the right words. There can be tremendous freedom in private recitation that is not available in communal recitation. In this we may recapture to a certain extent the prayers of those ancient hermits on Mount Carmel who prayed the psalms in solitude, listening to the Lord speak to them even as they uttered the words of the psalms to him.

There is nothing wrong with Lay Carmelites occasionally substituting something else for the Divine Office. On a given day, perhaps one might say the rosary instead of evening prayer, or a litany instead of one of the Little Hours. While the Divine Mercy Chaplet is not a Carmelite Prayer, there is no need to read afternoon prayer when we say the chaplet in mid-afternoon. A multitude of words does not make prayer. Good prayer gives the Lord's ears a break and his heart a workout. Perhaps on a given day we just want to page through our favourite psalms, or do a *lectio divina* on a Gospel passage. The point is not in following some regulation that does not, in any event, bind the laity but in giving yourself to prayer, particularly prayer that is reflective and rooted in the scriptures.

On the other hand, our communal recitation might need a bit of work. While a certain diversity of custom is good in how we say the Office, many communities have been poorly instructed and do not understand the basic structure of the Liturgy of the Hours. It would be helpful to have a set of flexible norms on when we might stand or sit or kneel and who is the appropriate person to say this prayer or do that reading. We certainly don't want to become rigid and rubrical, but there is a basic structure and flow to the Liturgy of the Hours that is best honoured if it is to be the prayerful experience it is meant to be. Nothing is worse than a rushed and perfunctory recitation of the Liturgy. We want to strike a balance between doing the Liturgy well and with dignity and giving ourselves time and energy for solitary prayer that flows from the Liturgy.

CHAPTER 12

Albert

None of you must lay claim to anything as your own, but you are to possess everything in common and each is to receive from the prior–that is from the brother he appoints for the purpose–whatever befits his age and needs. However, as I have said, each one of you is to stay in your allotted cell, and live by yourself on what is given out to you.

Pope Innocent IV (the 1247 revision)
None of the brothers must lay claim to anything as his own, but you are to possess everything in common; and each is to receive from the prior – that is from the brother he appoints for the purpose – whatever befits his age and needs.

This is a particularly interesting chapter. The hermits undoubtedly included some idea of common possession of goods in their proposal to Albert but this chapter actually shows evidence of Albert's authorship. Perhaps this chapter is his original composition, but more likely he rewrote this section of their proposal in his own style. It is not as evident in the English translation as it is in the Latin text, but Albert clearly borrowed from Acts 4:32 and Acts 4:35 in composing this passage. He does not quote directly, but Craig Morrison demonstrates that Albert clearly uses words and phrases lifted directly from the scripture to make his point about common goods. The Acts text says

"The community of believes was of one heart and mind, and no one claimed that any of his possessions was his own, but they had everything in common. ...they placed them (their possessions) at the feet of the apostles, and they were distributed to each according to his need."

Even in the English translation we can see the influence of the biblical text on Albert's instruction, but the Latin of the Rule matches the Latin of the scriptures so closely that its dependency cannot be ignored.

Now, as idealistic as this passage in Acts and in the Rule sounds, there is a shadow side to it. Luke, in Acts, makes it clear that while the community had voluntarily agreed to hold their property in common, not all were honest about this. Luke follows with the story of Ananias and his wife, Sapphira. They sold a piece of property and made a pretense of giving the Apostles the entire proceeds while, in fact, they held something back. In the Acts of the Apostles, the sin is clearly not in the holding back, for Peter tells Ananias that the property had belonged to them and was theirs to do as they wished. The sin was in the pretense of conforming to the community policy of contributing one's resources while in fact retaining private ownership. Albert does not comment on that, but Morrison implies it was on his mind. Certainly there are those who talk about community but think first of themselves. There are those who take plenty from the community and give little in return–not only materially but in every respect. Albert was himself a seasoned Religious. He knew that community life is not always what we profess it to be. There are givers and there are takers.

In the decades after Albert wrote this *Pattern for Life* for the hermits, clarifications were made regarding poverty. A very strict Franciscan style poverty was imposed on the community by Pope Gregory IX, who had been the friend and admirer of Francis of Assisi, Cardinal Ugolino, and who was, at the time, in communication with Saint Clare about the very issue of poverty. The Church was reluctant to allow the Franciscan women to live without property and income. They were, after all, cloistered nuns. They could not go and beg alms if needed for their survival as the friars could. If they had no food, they might literally starve. Clare, however, argued that she and her nuns wanted the "privilege of poverty" that Francis had mandated for his followers. She trusted in God's providence and in fact made a brilliant connection between poverty and the contemplative vocation of the nuns. It was precisely their dependency on God, she said, not on property or income, that would keep them focused on prayer. When Gregory wrote the hermits on Mount Carmel he used Clare's argument to tell them why they were not to own property or houses but live totally dependent on God and thus preserve their contemplative vocation.

Alas, the highest ideals fall first. It was not long before the Carmelites began accepting not only the ownership of property, but of investments and incomes. Their poverty has been mitigated over the years. At times they have even built huge churches and monasteries, living like gentlemen rather than like apostles. At the same time, other friars have gone off to mission stations of the most dire poverty or worked with the poorest of the poor in the cities of Europe and the Americas sharing their plight. Individual friars and nuns often live extremely simply even when their communities have considerable comfort available. Similarly the monasteries of nuns are usually very spartan and devoid of any unnecessary luxury. The various congregations of Carmelite Sisters do some remarkable work with the poor, especially in places such as East Timor, Zimbabwe, and Brazil where the poverty can be overwhelming. But in the end, poverty is one of the hardest things to regulate because it involves virtue and law can never mandate virtue, only grace inspires virtue.

LAY CARMELITES AND THE RULE, CHAPTER 12.

It is not practical, of course, for people in the lay life to commit themselves either to a radical poverty that would leave them without the proper amount of financial security or, save in some exceptional circumstances, a community of goods in which private ownership is renounced in favor of a Christian form of communal ownership and interdependent living. It is for this reason that Lay Carmelites do not make a promise or a vow of "poverty." (Incidentally, the Religious vow poverty to renounce their natural right to private ownership, not poverty in the sense of destitution. Albert calls the vow the "abdication of private property" in the Latin text of his *Formula Vitae*. Destitution or the lack of basic requirements for living in dignity is never a Christian virtue.) Nonetheless, all Carmelites–and indeed all Christians–need to consider how to simplify their lifestyle and mature beyond the psychological compulsion to possess more than we need. As we grow in the spiritual life, our hearts, by grace, should settle on what we need to fulfill God's plan in our lives (The Kingdom of God) and become free of superfluous attachment and desire. We also need to mature in a sense of stewardship in which we realize that what we "have" we, in fact, do not possess. The prophet Job is right–we are born naked and we die naked. Whatever we have we did not come into the world with and we do not take out of the world. It is only ours for the use. And the challenge is to use what we have been given as good stewards who will one day render account of what God has entrusted to us.

Part of this sense of stewardship is to realize our obligations to the larger Carmelite family. We should, as far as we are able, support the work of the Third Order both in our local communities and on the provincial levels. Some Lay Carmelites complain about the annual dues, though no one may ever be turned away because they cannot afford the membership. But instead of complaining, there are others who are always looking to see what they can do to help the local community–buying books for its library, bringing refreshments for the meeting, contributing towards bringing in speakers or sending members to conferences or workshops. Similarly, there are those who make contributions above and beyond the dues to the provincial offices of the Lay Carmelites to help defray the cost of the ministry. It may surprise you, it always did me, that the Lay Carmelites do not pay for themselves in some provinces. Instead of being a resource to the Friars and their mission, the Lay Carmelite ministry often requires subsidies from the Friars to cover the expenses of the Lay Carmelite Administration. Fortunately there are some who make a contribution or leave a bequest in their will that help make up this difference from time to time.

Lay Carmelites have an obligation, as to all Carmelites, to support the work of the Order in both material and spiritual ways. This means that they should assist the cloistered Nuns, including the Discalced Nuns, the Religious Sisters, and the Friars. The Carmelite missions are a particular area where support is appreciated, as are the funds for the training of students and the retirement of the elderly Religious. The spirit of the Acts of the Apostles should make us generous with the larger community to which we belong.

Many Catholics today have learned to follow the biblical injunction to tithe. It often requires stepping out in faith to give 10% of our income to God and his work, but it is a stepping out that will always be rewarded both spiritually and materially. The Catholic practice of tithing generally suggests that 5% be given to one's parish and 5% to other Catholic or worthy charitable causes. Part of this second 5% might go the local diocesan charity appeal, for example, or to support a Catholic school. We might think of giving one of those second five percent to Carmelite charities. This means that we would dedicate 1% of our income to the Lay Carmelites, to the Nuns, or to the work of the Friars. It would be a good way, however symbolic, to participate in the Rule's injunction that we are to hold all things in common. Nothing befits a Christian less well than possessiveness or stinginess. Jesus reminds us that the measure with which we give is the measure with which we shall receive.

CHAPTER 13

Pope Innocent IV (the 1247 revision)
You may have as many asses and mules as you need, however, and may keep a certain amount of livestock or poultry.

As is indicated in the italic print, this chapter is an addition to the Rule by Pope Innocent IV's commission when they took Albert's *Pattern for Life* and made it a Rule. It reflects the changed situation of the hermits who are no longer a single community of lay hermits but an international Order of mendicant friars. The pope permits them asses and mules for a purpose. They have to travel. They are founding new communities. Friars are travelling from one community to another on business for the Order. Asses and mules are how they travel–not only riding on them, indeed they probably walked more than they rode–but using the animals to carry books, vestments, sacred vessels, and other goods needed in the new monasteries. The animals also were needed as beasts of burden by the friars in the construction of their new monasteries and in the work in the monastery garden and its simple farming tasks. The same is true for the livestock and poultry. Chickens or ducks provided eggs, sheep and cows provided milk, cheese, butter, and cream. It was normal in the Middle Ages, even the cities, for people to keep some animals for food. The Carmelite Friars were not permitted to eat meat, but that made eggs and dairy all the more important for a balanced diet.

It should be noted that the pope granted the Carmelites the use of asses and mules and not horses. Horses were for the nobility and the rich. Not only friars but even great prelates were supposed to ride asses or mules in imitation of Christ who rode a humble animal into Jerusalem, not a proud beast. Furthermore, the horse was an animal of war. It was proper to the knight. The ass or the mule is an animal of peace, symbolized by Our Lord's riding an ass into Jerusalem on Palm Sunday when he fulfilled the prophecy of the Peaceful King (Zechariah 9:9) The clergy were supposed to renounce violence and warfare–that was the duty of the knightly class. Unfortunately, many churchmen in the Middle Ages preferred to ride the more elegant horse than the humble mule. Human nature does not change much over the centuries.

Lay Carmelites and the Rule, Chapter 13.

This chapter may seem somewhat antiquated to us today but it still tells us something important. It tells us that we may have what we need for our work. In North America, and some other places in the developed world, the Friars have found it important that each have a car for his use. This would have been an extravagance even in the United States just a generation ago, but we have found that if a friar did not have access to a car his work was hampered. We live in a very mobile society and we need to be able to go where we are needed and to go quickly. Even in developing countries it is important that the Friars or Carmelite Sisters have sufficient means of travelling to reach their various mission stations. And we need safe vehicles, in as good repair as we can have them. But we do not need flashy vehicles. It requires honesty for us to consider truthfully the differences between what is a genuine need and what is a frivolous desire. Furthermore, this applies not only to cars or trucks, but to other things we need to do the portion of God's work that is assigned to us. Computers, internet access, books, and probably most valuable of all, time, needs to be given us to the measure that our work requires. Even the needs for things like clothing differ according to our work. A Carmelite who lectures at a university has different needs for books and need of different clothing than a Carmelite whose work keeps him in a library most of the day. A friar who is parish priest in a rural parish has different needs than a friar who studying for his doctorate in Rome. The important thing is not that we all have the same but that the needs of each are carefully discerned and provided for. As we mature in the spiritual life, however, we find that our true needs are fewer and fewer. That is something else we should consider. Psychologically, the needs of the older, and hopefully more mature, are less than the needs of the younger who are still learning to discern between genuine need and superfluous wants. It is sad to see an older Carmelite friar who still is entrapped by wanting the most stylish clothes or the flashiest car or eating at the most extravagant restaurants.

In the same way for Lay Carmelites, as we mature in the spiritual life we should see the vanity of so much of what we once valued. There is nothing wrong with a lovely home, with a pleasant vacation, with dressing well. But when we live for these things, when they attract our attention and consume our time, it is a sign that we are not maturing. In truth, the older we get, the less we need. As we mature, our lifestyle should slowly but certainly tone down–and at the same time we should be happy about that, finding contentment in using less rather than being agitated because we do not have more. It is a matter of seeing things for their true worth. That which does God's work has value. That which is not about God's work is irrelevant to God's servant. Have what you need to live well, but remember living well is not about comfort or style, it is about integrity. Have what you need to live well in the sight of God. And remember that in fact we have nothing to our own–we are but stewards of what God has entrusted to us to do his work. We were born without pockets and we will go to the grave without pockets. But the King will ask us to give an account of all that he has entrusted to us in the meantime.

CHAPTER 14

An oratory should be built as conveniently as possible among the cells, where, if it can be done without difficulty, you are to gather each morning to hear Mass.

This chapter tells us that the hermits did not have an oratory, a chapel, at the time that Albert approved their *Pattern for Life*. That means that up until this point they did not have a place in which they could celebrate Mass and therefore had to leave the hermit colony and go to a church for Mass. This again indicates that there was no sort of enclosure on the original community. Enclosure in the sense that it is used among Carmelite Nuns–and other orders of enclosed nuns–was unknown to the hermits. Indeed even monastic communities, both of men and women, did not practice enclosure in the sense that we are familiar with it. Enclosure of nuns was mandated by Pope Boniface VIII in 1298 in the Bull *Periculoso*, but, to be honest, it was honoured more in the breach than in the observance through most of the Middle Ages. It is only after the Council of Trent that it is enforced–and even then with difficulty–on all communities of vowed women. In the Middle Ages monastic communities kept an enclosure in the sense that the interior of the monastic precincts–the refectory, the chapter room, the calefactory, the library, the courtyards and their arcades (cloisters), the choir of the church, and of course the dormitories, were supposed to be restricted to the Religious. But there were parlours where the Religious could speak with visitors–without grilles and barriers–and the Religious were permitted to walk around the outer precincts with guests and visitors. Guests would be entertained in the guest hall or at the Abbot's house where the monks, or in the case of women's communities, the nuns, could visit as well. Furthermore, monks and nuns would leave the precincts and travel as needed on Church or State business. Indeed, Chaucer's prioress and her companion go quite freely on pilgrimage to Canterbury a century after Boniface had insisted on confining them to their cloister. It is only after Trent that a different practice of enclosure for nuns is enforced than for monks. For lay hermits, invariably men in the Middle Ages, there was no cloistering. Mendicant friars also came and went from their convents as were required by the needs of the apostolate, and unfortunately at times, as their social lives required as well. Access to the dormitories in the friaries and abbeys was restricted, but the cloister arcades, the chapter room, and even the refectory were often used by various lay groups and civic associations for meetings. One of the most dramatic instances of this is that the Chapter House of the Monks of Westminster was the ordinary meeting place for "The King's Great Council" or Parliament from the fourteenth through the sixteenth century.

Another unusual element about this matter of enclosure is that Albert told the hermits to build the oratory in the middle of the cells. In traditional monastic architecture, the oratory or Church was built at the edge of the precincts, allowing the laity to access it from outside and the Religious to access it from their restricted precincts. Theoretically the monastic precincts were off limits to any but the monks, and this was usually true in women's monasteries, but as was just pointed out in the example of Westminster Abbey, this was less often enforced in men's communities. Albert curiously expressed no such concerns about restricting access to the site of the hermitages. He wanted the oratory plunk in the middle of the cells which means that as pilgrims made their way to the hermits' oratory they would be walking amidst the cells of the hermits. And we know that pilgrims did come to the oratory–the hermits asked the Holy See to grant indulgences to those pilgrims who make the slight detour from the Jerusalem road to visit their settlement. So again we see that these hermits were not enclosed. The prior does have guard over the gate to regulate the entrance of visitors, but there is no indication that he kept them out. Indeed everything about the site indicates they were very welcome. When the hermits built their grand monastery in the 1260's–and probably abandoned the hermitages at the same time to live in the monastery–they constructed a grand reception room at ground level and then an elegantly curved stairway to bring visitors from the entrance level to the higher terrace behind where the oratory stood. Any romantic ideas of enclosure on Mount Carmel should probably be abandoned. These hermits were very much engaged with the pilgrims going from Acre to Jerusalem. This should not surprise us as the care of pilgrims was a common service rendered by lay hermits.

Now in all this fuss about enclosure, we don't want to overlook the point of the chapter which is the daily Mass. Daily Mass was common practice among Religious communities by the thirteenth century. Indeed the great monastic communities usually had two and even three Masses in their schedule of daily Offices–the daily conventual Mass, a second Mass in honour of Our Lady, and a third for the faithful departed. Nevertheless, the eminent Rules–that of Benedict and Augustine–as well as the newer Rules such as that which Francis prepared for his friars in 1222 never mention the frequency of Mass being celebrated. Albert's *Pattern for Life*, on the other hand, made the daily Mass a central feature of the hermits' life.

When Albert's *Pattern for Life* treats the Mass, however, it is not with the same understanding that we have in the Catholic Church after Vatican II. Albert tells the hermits that "*ad audienda Missarum sollemnia convenire debeatis*"–they should gather for the solemn hearing of Masses. They are to *hear* Mass. The theology of the Eucharist is the medieval understanding of the priest offering the Mass on behalf of the congregation. The role of the faithful was to hear the Mass–that is to be attentively present at Mass. But this does not mean that they are simply to be passive for Albert mandates the *solemn* hearing of Mass. This implies not the quiet prayer of the low Mass, but a fully developed and celebrated liturgy. It would imply that the Mass is being celebrated by at least a priest and deacon, if not a full complement of ministers. It would also imply the chants of the Mass being sung. The rite used in the Holy Land was the Rite of the Church of the Holy Sepulchre which was a very rich rite with many exotic feasts and more ritual than the very sober Roman Rite of the pre-Tridentine era. In a relatively small community of hermits this would require considerable participation by all. Father Elias Friedman wrote in his study of the Latin Hermits that the size of the community can be estimated by the size of the stone bench that ran along the wall of the oratory. The original oratory was approximately 12 meters long and 6 meters wide (40' x 20'), allowing room for a community between 25 and 30 when one subtracts sanctuary area. Most likely, the original community was a bit smaller, planning a chapel that would accommodate their needs as they grew. In fact, by the 1260's they needed to double the size of the oratory. By the time you have your priest and deacon, and possibly, at least for greater feasts, subdeacon and archpriest, a complement of servers, and a small choir for the chants just about everyone is involved. This would be a rather interactive group during their daily gathering for prayer.

What would be most strange to us, however, is that probably only the celebrant normally received Holy Communion. Daily communion was not the practice in the Church until the reforms of Pope Saint Pius X at the beginning of the twentieth century. In the early thirteenth century many people, most people in fact, received Holy Communion only once a year. Judging from the thirteenth century constitutions of various Religious Communities, most religious probably received Holy Communion between seven and ten times a year, most probably at the first Sunday of Advent, Christmas, the Purification of the Virgin Mary, Holy Thursday, Easter Day, Pentecost, the Assumption of the Virgin, the Nativity of the Virgin, and All Saints day. The oldest known set of Carmelite Constitutions, dating from 1281, requires seven annual communions.

Lay Carmelites and the Rule, Chapter 14.

The most important point of this chapter is the reminder that the Eucharist is central in our lives and that we should participate in the Mass daily if at all possible. Our appreciation of the Eucharist is to be a contemporary appreciation of course, not the same understanding as the hermits had in the thirteenth century. By the Middle Ages many in the Church, especially on the popular level, had lost the rich and deep appreciation of the Eucharistic mystery that is present in both the Scripture and the Church Fathers. While they retained, and even grew in appreciation for, the understanding of Christ's Real Presence in the Eucharist, medieval Christians had too often lost an appreciation for the intrinsic link that both Saint Paul and the Fathers, especially Saint Augustine, make between the Eucharistic Presence of Christ and the nature of the

Church as the Body of Christ. Scholarship of the nineteenth and twentieth century as well as majestic teaching of Pius XII in his encyclical letter *Mystici Corporis* and the decrees of the Second Vatican Council have helped us recover an understanding that the Eucharistic Presence of Christ cannot be separated from his Presence in his Body the Church of which we are each members. Thus for us the horizontal bonds of fraternal charity are an intrinsic part of our vertical ties of adoration of the Father through the Son. Also, ever since Pope Saint Pius X began the liturgical reforms of the twentieth century, reforms that matured in the *Novus Ordo* liturgy of Pope Paul VI, and which are continuing to mature and be refined in these years after the Council, we have understood the importance of active participation by all the faithful in the liturgy. We know that we cannot be passive participants in the liturgical worship of God but that we are called to a full and active participation in whatever ministries the Church calls us to–as readers, musicians, ministers of hospitality, extraordinary ministers of the Eucharist, servers, sacristans, deacons, or priests. Indeed, we have come to appreciate our role that the scriptures define for us as a priestly people, actively offering to God our intercession for the needs of the Church, the poor, the suffering, and indeed the whole world. We join with Christ our High Priest in making intercession before the Throne of Grace, not only in the Mass but in the Liturgy of the Hours and in private prayer,

Biblical and patristic scholarship has also helped us to appreciate more deeply the meaning of the Eucharistic sacrifice. We know that the Mass is a sacrifice in as that in the Eucharist we become present to the one eternally timeless sacrifice which Christ has offered and eternally offers at Calvary. There is no sacrifice apart from the Cross, but the Cross stands forever beyond time and in the Eucharist we too stand beyond time and place caught momentarily into Eternity joined with Christ who is both eternal Priest and eternal Victim. And we come to appreciate too that our participation in this one eternal sacrifice is a participation in which we join ourselves to Christ, conform ourselves to Christ, so that it is no longer we who live but Christ Jesus who lives in us. We die with Christ in order to be raised as members of his body and so we to find ourselves being conformed to the obedience of Christ, mirroring in our obedience to the Divine Will his obedience to the Divine Will. In this way we are called to surrender all that we are and all that we have to the Father. United to Christ in his sacrifice, our lives too are offered to God. It is not bread and wine that we bring to God for he has no more use of bread and wine than he had of the blood of goats and bulls in the time of the Temple and its sacrifices. It is contrite and humbled hearts that God desires. The bread and wine are shadows of ourselves and all that we have–we offer who we are and what we have to the Father and he transforms us into Christ. And so the question comes to us–when we come away from the Eucharist, are we transformed? Have we become Christ? Have we become perfectly obedient to the Father? Have we been transformed into incarnate love for a loveless world? The bitter shock is how imperfect our offering has been, how we have in fact held back and not given our all. But this Eucharist for us is not a few comfortable minutes with our Lord in the privacy of our hearts; it is a full and frightening entry into the Holy of Holies where we come face to face with the awesome perfection of God and our wretched selfishness that separates us from him. But with lives of prayer we believe that with each encounter with the Divine Majesty in the Eucharistic Sacrifice, with each ingesting of Christ in his body and blood, we become more and more conformed to him. We may fall short of all we hope to become, but by his grace with each encounter we fall less short and Christ grows more and more in us. The only measuring stick of this transformation, however, is our growth in charity for it is by charity that we know that we are his disciples.

The other aspect we should consider is that our celebration of the Eucharist is never a private affair. The oratory was in the midst of the cells. The hermits were not sequestered away for private devotions. So too we Lay Carmelites celebrate in the middle of the world, in the heart of the Church. Aside from the Nuns–who are cloistered because they are women, not because they are Carmelites–we Carmelites are not enclosed in any sense. The world freely comes to us and we freely go to the world. When the world comes to us we offer them Christ, when we go into the world we bring Christ–and as we mature spiritually we realize that we find Christ already there, we recognize him in the most improbable places and situations. We have a positive and open attitude towards the world in which we live. We know that the Father created it, the Son has redeemed it, and the Holy Spirit sanctifies it. We reject not this world which God has made, redeemed and sanctified, but the corruption of God's goodness that human sinfulness, our sinfulness, distorts from the perfection for which God has destined the world. As Carmelites we want always to be opening and welcoming to whomever stops by our place of prayer as they pass by on their particular pilgrim journey.

CHAPTER 15

On Sundays too, or other days if necessary, you should discuss matters of discipline and your spiritual welfare; and on this occasion the indiscretions and failings of the brothers, if any be found at fault, should be lovingly corrected.

This is a very wise prescription whether it was from Albert or part of the hermits' original proposal. It is remarkable when you consider it because the hermits had very little time together, normally just morning Mass, and yet they are to have a weekly gathering where they discuss the issues before them–ranging from the broad vision of spiritual welfare to the narrow petty annoyances that we all find when we have to live with others. Furthermore, they are to discuss matters of discipline and spiritual welfare, the implication being that the prior will not unilaterally decide these things but that the community will have an opportunity to reflect together.

Another remarkable item in this is Albert, or whoever is the author, presumes that it is possible to get through a week without any of the brothers displaying any indiscretions or failings. This is a notably positive anthropology. In later periods we have always presumed that one could not go a week without sin, much less with out some fault or failing showing.

By bringing the community together for honest conversation about their goals and vision for life and with an opportunity to confront disruptive behaviour, an important safety valve is built into the Rule. The hermits, or perhaps later the friars, interpreted this chapter to conform to the monastic practice of the Chapter of Faults. Again, often a negative anthropology foreign to Albert crept in because if no one confessed any fault or failing, or accused another of any fault or failing, during the previous week, the suspicion would have been that something was being covered up. People were all but obliged to confess and some were always quick to accuse.

The practice of the Chapter of Faults has died out in the post-Conciliar Church, probably because of the Jansenist corruption it had undergone, but it might be advisable to resurrect it if it could be carried out in a constructive way.

The final observation, which is quite obvious really, is that the correction is to be carried out in charity. When we hear the stories of "the days of the giants" or "the good old days" that admonition about faults being corrected in charity again is something that seems more often to have been honoured in the breach than the observance.

Lay Carmelites and the Rule, Chapter 15

Good leadership in the community will keep the focus of the community's meetings on spiritual growth and let neither items of business nor idle chatter take our attention from what is truly important. Furthermore, while the community might often invite in speakers to address them on matters of spirituality, the format will always allow for discussion on the part of the community as to how they might take the insights and apply them. The discussion, in fact, is more important than the talk. The input should be primarily to focus and energize the members of the community to appropriate the material for themselves.

It is also important that whatever input is used in the meetings to stimulate discussion of spiritual growth be focused on our Carmelite heritage and consistent with the teaching and discipline of the Church. This is not the occasion to invite one's favourite priest to come and talk about whatever interests him, but rather because such talks both provide input and stimulate discussion, they are an essential part of the ongoing formation of the community and they should follow some carefully planned program of spiritual formation. There are many fine–and some not so fine–speakers in the Church today who can talk about a wide variety of subjects from the Liturgy to Stem-Cell Research, from Magisterial Authority to saintly incorruptibles. Most of these topics do not belong at a gathering of the Lay Carmelite community.

The leadership also needs to find the most constructive ways to defuse tensions in the community. Tension cannot be swept under the rug, it will not stay there. Sometimes tension needs to be brought out into the open and confronted openly. Sometimes, more often probably, it needs to be defused by private conversations–and admonitions–behind the scene. If it looks like it will get out of control, the Regional Coordinator or the Provincial Office should be consulted before it becomes problematic for the entire community. Once the genie is out of the bottle, the damage is done. When individuals are disruptive with any degree of consistency this needs to be dealt with squarely. It will normally surface during a person's probationary period and a person who is disruptive in the community should not be allowed to continue in the formation process. This sometimes takes "some guts" on the part of the leadership, but in the long-term will save the community grief. The Religious in the Order have long known that not everyone who comes seeking admission belongs. Of course we must distinguish between those who are disruptive and those who are identifying dysfunction in the community. However, if the problem is not the individual but the community or the leadership of the community, healthy individuals will not want to stay and will leave anyway. The Provincial Office quickly becomes aware of which communities are dysfunctional or have dysfunctional leadership. It is more difficult to deal with a disruptive person who is in final promises or vows than it is with a candidate in initial formation, but even here we can ask an individual not to attend the meetings if they do not stay within the bounds of constructive behaviour. If they are being treated unjustly in this request, the Provincial Office can mediate the dispute. In mature communities that are keeping their focus on the spiritual maturity of their members these problems should be rare. Spirituality, at least authentic spirituality, provides a common ground for people of diverse opinions to meet and share, respecting the experience of Grace in others and being slow to judge their brothers or sisters except by the volume of charity they manifest in their lives.

There is a need that we avoid being caught in some of the controversies that are plaguing the Church at the popular level and the best way to do this is to keep our focus on our Carmelite spiritual tradition. It is disconcerting how many people consider themselves experts these days in theology or liturgy but who have no formal training, just strong opinions. People who want to bring controversy into our communities are not doing us a favour and should not be encouraged to stay. The Religious in Carmel have learned to live with a certain indifference to varying customs and traditions and be tolerant of other opinions in the non-essentials. Carmelite Laity too must keep the focus which is on spiritual maturing at the service of the Church and in faithfulness to the Gospel.

Chapter 16

You are to fast every day, except Sundays, from the feast of the Exaltation of the Holy Cross until Easter Day, unless bodily sickness or feebleness, or some other good reason, demand a dispensation from the fast; for necessity overrides every law.

Every Religious Rule has certain prescriptions regarding the practice of fasting and there is considerable variance depending on the dietary needs required to sustain a particular lifestyle. The *Pattern for Life* that Albert gave the hermits presupposed a rather sedentary and agricultural life. It was the same fast, basically, as outlined in the Rule of Benedict for his monks. (Benedict told his monks to fast from the Ides of September, September 15, until Easter. The Feast of the Holy Cross, September 14, was not yet established when Benedict wrote his Rule.) This fast was not only of religious significance, but had a practical side to it. It allowed extra food during the heaviest season of agricultural labour–the spring field work through the harvest in late summer and early fall. It also structured food conservation through the winter.

Albert does not spell out the specifics of the fast. Possibly different hermits adjusted the fast to their own spiritual needs, some perhaps fasting more severely than others. This would be especially true if, as some historians surmise, the hermits had been gathered together from different communities that had existed before the Battle of Hattin but were unable to reorganize at their old sites after Saladin's conquests. Different communities would have minor variations in fasting, especially where there may have been some influence from the Eastern Churches and their disciplines which varied considerably from one another as well as from the Latin practices.

Note that there is no Sunday fast. The ancient custom of the Church did not allow Sunday fasting as Sunday, every Sunday, is a celebration of the Resurrection of the Lord. Notice also that the fast does not obligate when it is damaging to our health or when there is another–and it is left undefined–good reason. Finally, note the prescription that necessity overrides every law, in the Latin original, necessity has no law.

Lay Carmelites and the Rule, Chapter 16

Fasting should be part of our life. Our fast should be tied in some way to keeping in our minds the cycle of the Lord's life–fasting in times of penance, feasting in times of celebration. Our fast also should be practical, useful to our health and suited to our needs. It is not meant to be a burden but a discipline. God takes no pleasure in human discomfort (and is never pleased with anything that damages our health). But moderate discipline keeps us mindful–mindful of the liturgical season, mindful of the needs of those who have less, and mindful of our own bodies and their welfare. Albert does not spell out the specifics of the fast and this permits us variation to our own spiritual needs as it may have permitted a certain variation among the hermits. We are used to the principle of two light meals that together do not equal the third normal meal on a fast day. This is a modern invention. Medieval people did not typically eat three meals a day as we do.

There were often two meals, a heavier meal in the late morning and a light meal in the evening. The Eastern Church traditionally measures the fast more by the avoidance of certain foods–in addition to meat, the rejection of any dairy, and for some the rejection of oil. We are free to plan our fast in whatever way is most helpful to us. For some, fasting may not even involve food. It may be an abstinence from alcohol or smoking. It may be the avoidance of television or internet time. The discipline of fasting should revolve around an area into which we need to bring more discipline into our lives. That need for discipline, and thus the form of our fasting, will change periodically as one vice is tamed and, to our dismay, another springs up. Nevertheless, the fasting from certain foods or the restriction of our diet within the limits of good health management is the more normal sort of fast and one from which most of us can benefit.

We should not fast on Sundays or the great feasts of the Church. The Rule is explicit on this point. The spiritual life is not a contest in which we strive to outdo others in our rigor. Feasting on certain days–and within appropriate boundaries–is as important as fasting on other days. Saint Teresa of Avila's famous adage applies: there is a time for penance and a time for partridge! The feast, as well as the fast, keeps us aware of the sacredness of time. The prohibition of a Sunday fast, which is contained in the explicit exemption of Sunday from the fast, might actually be an encouragement for us to revive the important custom of Sunday dinner as a time to gather family and guests together. There was a point to the custom of Sunday Dinner. When the Lord's Day was still sacred, Sunday was Church and Dinner. They were seen as related activities. Sunday dinner should be an extension of the Sunday Eucharist and a reminder that Sunday, every Sunday, is a celebration of the Lord's Resurrection.

CHAPTER 17

Albert
You are always to abstain from meat, unless it has to be eaten as a remedy for sickness or great feebleness.

Pope Innocent IV (the 1247 revision)
You are to abstain from meat, except as a remedy for sickness or feebleness. But as, when you are on a journey, you more often than not have to beg your way; outside your own houses you may eat foodstuffs that have been cooked with meat, so as to avoid giving trouble to your hosts. At sea, however, meat may be eaten.

Albert imposed a total abstinence from meat on the hermits. This is a curiously severe restriction. While Carthusians practiced total abstinence from meat, the Rule of Benedict permitted fowl. Most of the "new orders" of the thirteenth century did not impose abstinence for various reasons. Francis intended his friars to be so dependent on alms that he was anxious to permit them to eat whatever was given them. Dominic and his friars were combating a heresy, Catharism or the Albigensian heresy, which taught that eating the products of animal copulation (both meat and dairy) was sinful. The Dominicans, to prove their orthodoxy and establish that they were in fact not part of this heretical movement which they resembled for their white robes and their poverty, placed no restriction on meat in their diet beyond the normal custom of the Church. Although meat was expensive and thus, except for the nobility, fairly rare in the medieval diet, by the thirteenth century most urban people would have had some meat in their diet several days a week. Certainly in the Holy Land what meat that was available formed an important part of most people's diet. Thus the imposition of total abstinence on the hermits was shockingly severe. On the other hand, their hermitage was within site of the sea and fish offered a reasonable nutritional substitute for meat. Notice, of course, that health needs exempted a hermit from the abstinence.

By the time of Innocent IV, the severity already required a mitigation. The situation had changed. The Carmelites were no longer a single community of hermits living by the sea, but a growing network of communities scattered from the Holy Land to England. Travel was a normal part of life for many of them as went on business from one house to another, often travelling by sea. Innocent made it clear that the law was not to be a burden. While travelling on land they should not eat meat, but they could eat food cooked with meat. A common part of the medieval diet was *pulmentum*–a potage of vegetables kept simmering over the fire and into which, as the pot grew empty, new vegetables were tossed in a sort of never-ending vegetable stew, a pease porridge. However it was not vegetarian. Meat would also be thrown in and as it simmered would shred and fall off the bone and become part of the mix. This stew was usually highly flavoured and very much the staple of diet especially at inns or in establishments such as guest houses of Religious foundations where a kitchen, or at least a fireplace, was part of the establishment. It would have been impossible to eat the porridge without eating what meat was in it.

Sea travel was an entirely different matter. Salted or preserved meat was universal on the sea because it kept better than vegetables or other foods. Not to have eaten meat while travelling by sea would have required almost total starvation.

In the fifteenth century, there was further mitigation of the Rule when Eugene IV restricted the obligatory abstinence to Wednesdays, Fridays, and Saturdays–traditional fast days in the Church. Unlike the 1247 mitigation of Innocent IV, Pope Eugene did not change the text of the Rule, but simply issued a papal bull granting the mitigation. In fact, the friars had begun eating meat long before this restriction was lifted. Total abstinence from meat was found to be impractical and early on this chapter of the Rule was not seen to bind in any legalistic way. When the Prior General made a formal visit to Florence in 1387 he was served ducks, capons, sausages, lamb, and dried meats as well as other delicacies. There is no indication that he reproved the community for their lack of observance. He seems in fact to have eaten with gusto and to have reported the elegantly lavish table to his curia for the procurator general soon turned up and was entertained with only a slightly less sumptuous–and carnivorous–cuisine.

Various reforms of the Order, including the Reform of Saint Teresa, have always reinstituted the requirement of abstinence, renouncing the 1432 mitigation. Over the course of time, however, each of the Reforms has come to accept the mitigation. While a few monasteries of Discalced Carmelite Nuns still keep total abstinence from meat they are the exception even in their Order. In fact, several of those monasteries that keep it have petitioned for permission to eat meat but the local bishop, who is their ecclesiastical superior, has refused, not understanding this prescription in its historical context and often confusing rigorism with virtue. The Nuns often find the requirement to abstain from meat to be a heavy economic burden, especially as well-intentioned people often give them meat, not realizing that they cannot eat it. Fish is very expensive in most parts of the world, and while the Rule prohibits meat but does not mandate fish, for a balanced diet fish is a crucial source of low-fat protein. Of course for some of us, fish is also no penance, though for others it is a trial beyond endurance.

Lay Carmelites and the Rule, Chapter 17

This chapter should not be seen as binding in its literal sense as even the Religious do not consider it binding literally, and indeed have long seen its prohibition of meat as non-essential. To interpret it today might require us to think in several different ways.

The first way we might approach this is for the requirements for a regular diet that avoids extravagance. We might choose to ordinarily eat cheaply. This does not mean that we should not eat healthily however. We might plan meals that are low in fat, choosing white meats such as chicken or turkey over more expensive (and higher in fat) red meats. We might also think of cutting back on the amount of meat we eat, planning vegetarian meals several days a week or preparing dishes such as casseroles that use some meat but are primarily vegetables and grains. In any dish, however, we should think health. Similarly soups, even when based with a meat stock, can be a healthy and appropriate alternative. Hearty vegetable soups, dishes of chilli with beans, or meatless pastas are all alternatives.

Another way we might approach this is to discern what plays an important preference in our diet but is not necessarily good for us. We may choose to abstain from breads, or sweets, or butter. We may choose to drink our coffee without milk and sugar. A very good abstinence would be from sugared carbonated beverage such as soft-drinks, drinking water or fruit juices instead. Abstinence from alcohol is another form we might consider.

Whatever we do should be healthy and should be relative inconspicuous to others, even those of our own families. We might prepare a normal meal for the family, but choose a soup, a salad, or an omelette for ourselves without giving any pious reason for it. And whatever we do, we should not be rigid. There are exceptions to every Rule and as Teresa herself said, and as we have already quoted her–there is a time for penance, and a time for partridge. It might be particularly important that we do not give up meat altogether as if it becomes necessary at some point for us to eat meat–at a social occasion for example–we may find that even the smallest amount makes us ill. Our digestive track may not be able to handle it after prolonged abstinence. One of the problems we might face is that often when we make changes in our diet, even drastic ones, what begins as a penance often becomes a preference. When that happens, be sure to find a new penance to replace the new preference.

CHAPTER 18

Since man's life on earth is a time of trial, and all who would live devotedly in Christ must undergo persecution, and the devil your foe is on the prowl like a roaring lion looking for prey to devour, you must use every care to clothe yourselves in God's armour so that you may be ready to withstand the enemy's ambush.

This chapter marks a significant change in direction in the text. We are moving to a very different style of writing that indicates that perhaps there is a new author at work here. Indeed that new author could well be Albert himself as Father Craig Morrison's detailed study of Albert's use of scripture in the Rule shows how the very sophisticated use of scriptural texts attributed to the patriarch is typified in this and subsequent passages in ways in which it had only occasionally been present in the earlier chapters.

In this passage, Albert takes Job 7:1, 2 Timothy 3:12. 1 Peter 5:8, and Ephesians 6:11 and weaves them seamlessly together to produce a coherent and consistent thought that sets the stage for what I believe is the main point of Albert's letter to the hermits. It is a brilliant pastiche of scripture. The battle lies before us; we should not be surprised for our whole life is a struggle. But since our enemy is no one less than the Evil One, we must clothe ourselves in the only armour which can protect us from the devil–the armour of God himself.

No doubt that many in the hermits' day saw the enemy as Saladin and his Muslim army that had seized the Jerusalem holy places from the Christian crusaders. It was Islam and its armies that threatened Christianity–in the Holy Land, at the borders of the Byzantine Empire, in Spain and Portugal, on the frontiers of Christian Europe. The enemy had a face, and a scimitar. But Albert saw through that. Enemies, in fact, come and go–but the Enemy, the Evil One whose plan it is to destroy humankind in conflict and division and violence, that Enemy remains. Enemies can be defeated, they vanish from history as do all kingdoms and empires and nations, but the Enemy remains in each generation to work for the destruction of God's most hoped-filled Creation, the human family. The destiny which God has planned for us is the delight of the Evil One to destroy. The ancient monks in the desert knew this. They had always spoken of how our life here was a battle, a struggle, a time of testing. It was not God who desired us to be put to the test, it is the Evil One who sees in our sin-flawed nature an opportunity to thwart the divine plan. And so the life of the Christian, the life of the desert monk, the life of the hermit, the life of the faithful servant, is always one of resisting the Evil One, but that is a resistance that is only possible if we clothe ourselves in the armour which God offer us, his own strength.

Albert undoubtedly looked at the Holy Land of his day and saw the dismal failure of the crusades. He knew the Crusaders could not hold the land forever. They were greatly outnumbered. Their only hope in winning the land for Christ was to win the hearts of the people of the land to Christ, and that could only be done if the Christians, instead of trusting in their weapons and armour of war, trusted in God's armour and weapons. They needed to clothe themselves in the righteousness of God, not in earthly power. People would come to Christ if they could see the difference that Christianity makes in the lives of its believers.

The religious movements of the 12th and 13th centuries were all about trying to live the Gospel of Christ in daily life. Albert wanted these hermits to be people who took Christ at his Word and followed his Gospel. This was the way to defeat the enemy. Violence only begat violence, but the Gospel of Christ is the seed of the Kingdom of God. From the Gospel of Christ comes a rich harvest of righteousness and peace.

Albert was not the first to see that the monastic or hermit vocation was especially to be this sort of spiritual warfare. John Cassian had spoken to his monks in the fifth century of their need to take up the armour of God in the ascetical life (*Collatio* VII, number 5). Albert uses the idea in a very different context however and probably does not draw his inspiration from Cassian.

LAY CARMELITES AND RULE, CHAPTER 18

At the end of the nineteenth century an Indian-born but British educated attorney mounted the steps of a Protestant church in South Africa where he was living at the time. During his years at university in England, he had read about Christianity and found himself attracted to the teachings of Jesus. He studied the New Testament and he was curious about becoming a Christian. But at the doors of the church he was challenged by one of the church's elders–"where do you think you're going, kaffir?" (Kaffir is an ethnic slur used by whites in South Africa for people of colour.) The attorney replied that he would like to attend worship in the church. The elder told him "there's no room for kaffirs in this church. Get out of here or I'll have my assistants throw you down the steps." The man turned and walked away, away from the Church and away from Christianity. The man was Mohandas Gandhi, one of the great political and spiritual figures of the twentieth century.[11] What if he had come into

---

[11] The story is found on the webpage of John Mark Ministries, but its historical accuracy cannot be confirmed by any Ghandi biographies which I have found. It does correspond, however, to several remarks which Gandhi made about his admiration for Christ and his disappointment in Christians.

the Christian faith? How different would India be? How different would our world be? We can never know, of course, but it should give us pause to think.

The historical accuracy of the previous story, taken from an internet web-site by evangelical Christians, cannot be ascertained. I have searched biographies of Gandhi and have seen references to some such incidence but no clear ratification of the historicity of the story. The point remains none the less. If Christianity has failed to win the world for Christ, is it because we Christians have failed to live the Gospel of Christ? In the ancient world many came to Christianity because they saw not only the faithfulness of Christians in persecution, but because they saw the ardour of their love for all, even their enemies. Jesus has told us: this is how all will know you are my disciples–that you love one another. (John 13:35) He also has told us:

"You have heard the adage: love your countryman, hate your enemies. But I tell you, love your enemies, pray for your persecutors." (Matthew 5:43-44.)

Albert wanted the hermits to undertake the battle that the Crusades had lost. They could win the land for Christ if they took Christ at his Word. We too can win the world for Christ, if we take him at his Word. There are many today who believe our enemy is Islam. Twenty years ago it was Soviet Communism. Seventy years ago it was Nazi Germany. Before that it had been the Kaiser. At various times our enemy has been Protestantism (or, in England and the United States, the Pope was often seen as the enemy who was plotting the destruction of our good Protestant nations.) Jews were seen as the enemy, atheists, French Radicals. It gets ridiculous after awhile. Our only enemy is, was, and always has been the Evil One. Any earthly foe can be won over by the love of Christ. The only problem is that we have to believe enough to trust the love of Christ to be our only protection and our only weapon. Christ will draw all people to himself if we but let him use us in what is his battle.

CHAPTER 19

Your loins are to be girt with chastity, your breast fortified by holy meditations, for, as Scripture has it, holy meditation will save you. Put on holiness as your breastplate, and it will enable you to love the Lord your God with all your heart and soul and strength, and your neighbour as yourself. Faith must be your shield on all occasions, and with it you will be able to quench all the flaming missiles of the wicked one: there can be no pleasing God without faith; [and the victory lies in this – your faith]. On your head set the helmet of salvation, and so be sure of deliverance by our only Saviour, who sets his own free from their sins. The Sword of the Spirit, the Word of God, must abound in your mouths and hearts. Let all you do have the Lord's Word for accompaniment.

This is a truly fascinating chapter, and I believe the most crucial in the Rule. Remember in the prologue that Albert told us that he was writing to outline a way of life in which we could give allegiance to Jesus Christ? If we give him allegiance, then he, as our liege Lord, is pledged to give us salvation–and here we have it, we can "be sure of deliverance by our only Saviour, who sets his own free from their sins." This is the chapter that corresponds most directly to the earlier given point of Albert's project for Carmelites, a life of allegiance to Jesus Christ.

The first thing we might notice about the chapter is that it seems to be a quote from the sixth chapter of Paul's letter to the Ephesians, but when we look at it closely we notice that Albert has taken considerable liberties with the Ephesians text. The first liberty is in the very first sentence. Paul told the Ephesians to gird their loins in truth; Albert tells the hermits to gird their loins with chastity. In fact, by changing a key word, Albert underlines it. He stresses the importance of chastity by using it when the listener expects him to say "truth." He has reasons for stressing chastity, of course. In the first place, it was mentioned nowhere else in the *Pattern for Life* he gave the hermits. They only vowed obedience. The vow of chastity was not added until Innocent IV modified the *Pattern for Life* into a Rule in 1247. They understood, of course, that in their imitation of Christ they were to imitate him in his chastity as well as in his poverty and in his obedience. But this was an opportunity to stress that virtue. But it is more than that. It is their chastity, that they demonstrate their integrity. They are not simply pious people who have come to Carmel to meditate and pray. No, they are giving themselves 100% to the project. They are renouncing homes and families, wives and children and lives of their own, to follow Christ. These are no part-time spiritual warriors, but men who give their all in their allegiance to Jesus Christ. Truth and integrity are integrally related ideas. In fact, the truthfulness of these hermits, the totality of their dedication, will be witnessed to by their chastity.

Now when a soldier, in ancient Rome or in the Crusader times, dressed for battle, the first part of their body they protected was their loins. They did not want to leave themselves vulnerable to a spear or a sword or knife thrust up through their loins under their breastplate, and so they protected themselves with heavy leather padding. In the same way, it was chastity that offered these hermits protection where they might otherwise be vulnerable. Were they not chaste in heart as well as in body, they would have been vulnerable to the Evil One's attacks that could get in and pierce them beneath the breastplate of meditation and holy thoughts. Chastity is not primarily a matter of the body, but of the heart. Purity of body without a fundamental purity of spirit is no virtue, but leaves us cold, withdrawn, unable to love.

Then Albert tells them to fortify their breast with holy meditation. This is not in Paul, who does, however, speak of the breastplate of righteousness. Albert will get to that, but first the hermits are to fortify their breast with holy meditation. Again, the meditation is like the heavy leather padding that goes on beneath the armour. It not only gives extra protection, but in fact provides a foundation for the righteousness which will be the hermit's breastplate. Righteousness, sometimes translated justice or holiness–for the word in the scriptural text can be translated as any of the three–has to be founded on something. We don't just become right with God. Although such righteousness in the sight of God is a gift God gives us in his beloved Son, we have to grow into it. It is prayer, the reading of the scripture and the dwelling on that Word, which transforms our lives.

This is particularly important. Many people think of prayer as something they say or do, that is they hear "prayer" and think prayers. They say their prayers in the morning, they say their rosary, they read their novenas prayers, they may hear Mass, they say their bed-prayers at night. They may even read the Liturgy of the Hours. But prayer is always words they speak to God. But Albert here is telling the hermits not to say prayers, but to have meditation, literally–in this passage–holy thoughts. And such holy thoughts will save them he assures us. This by the way is taken from Proverbs, 2:11. It is only after they have prepared themselves with holy meditations that they can put on the breastplate of righteousness.

Now in the Latin this breastplate of righteousness, is the *lorica justiciae*. Righteousness and justice are synonymous in biblical language. In fact, holiness, righteousness, and justice are synonymous in the scriptures. We are holy when we are set right with God, and we are set right with God when our lives are ordered by justice. Albert wanted the hermits clothed not in any righteousness of their own–such armour would fail them in times of battle with the devil–but to be clothed in God's own armour. They are to put on the righteousness of Christ, the justice of Christ, the holiness of Christ.

So then the hermits would prepare themselves by meditation to put on Christ. By their meditation they would appropriate to themselves the very holiness of Christ, and this would empower them to love God with all their heart, all their strength, all their being. This meditation would also prepare them, and this is equally important, to love their neighbor. And this is how they would win the world for Christ–by being the very love of Christ in the world. The victory would be won, the land and its people would be won for Christ, by offering the world the example of those who love God with undivided hearts, and who fulfill the prophecy of Christ–that all know would know them to be his disciples by the love they have for one another. In loving God with their entire being and loving their neighbor as themselves, they would fulfill the commandment of Christ in Mark 12:30-31.[12] Who would be able to resist such witness as Christians who perfectly embodied the love which Christ commands?

Fortified with meditation, protected with holiness, they would then pick up the shield of faith and this faith would protect them against the flaming missiles of the Evil One. This passage is again taken directly from Ephesians 6, but Hebrews 11:6 is cited to remind us that there is no pleasing God without faith. It was, after all, not the good works of the hermits–their prayers, their labour, their penance–that pleased God,

---

[12] Of course Mark himself depends on to Deut 6,5 and Lev 19,18 to construct this double great-commandment.

but their faith. It is faith that sets us right with God. Paul leaves no doubt of that in his letters to the Romans or to the Galatians. Our prayers, our penances, our fasting, our works of charity–all these proceed from our lively and generous faith. They bear witnesses to our faith, but lives lived faithfully to the Gospel is what brings us salvation. The hermits were called to trust God, to put their faith in his Son and live according to the Gospel that his Son has given us. The Evil One can overcome all our good deeds but, while he can submit our faith to the test, he cannot overcome the gift of faith which we have received from God. We have only, by grace, to hold fast to our faith and the victory is ours. Our good works can be undone, turn to dust and ashes in our sight, but our faith–which is given to us by God–holds us firm against attack. We can see that in the terrible trials that Saint Thérèse underwent in her final months. Everything seemed worthless to her. In her trial of faith she saw how empty all her penances and prayers were. She knew that she ultimately went to God with empty hands, with nothing to show. And even her faith, perhaps especially her faith, was on trial–she could see only blackness when she looked into the future. But she remembered that faith is a gift from God and she clung to the tattered shreds of faith that were left her. So strange this trial of faith was that those around her had no idea of the inner torment she confided to her journals. After her death the other nuns, her physician, her relatives testified that they only saw peaceful serenity in her, charity never deserting her. As tormented as she was by doubt and fear, she clung to faith–faith that was not some passing feeling or sentiment, but faith that called her to faithfulness in the daily tasks of life, of loving God and loving neighbor with an undivided heart. Faith, after all does not mean that we do not doubt, even doubt profoundly. Faith means that we step out in obedience to God's command, giving 100%, taking no regard of the anxiety within, the weak knees, the lack of vision. Faith means that like Peter we step out of the boat onto the roiling seas, but unlike Peter we keep our eye fixed straight on Jesus, our hand reaching out to grasp his, as we walk towards him on the troubled waters of our lives. Against this sort of faith, the Evil One cannot prevail. He can rob us of our feelings and make the night dark and the waves high, but he cannot break our wills, as long as we hold the faith we have been given. The victory lies in this, Albert wrote the hermits, your faith.

And those hermits lived right on the edge. They were but a few miles from the Saracen lines. They lived there without walls and catapults and weapons to protect them. They went about their business, saying their prayers, keeping vigil in prayer at night, planting their gardens, welcoming the pilgrims. They lived in confidence that God would protect them, that he would be their all. They had no need of knights camped around their settlement, or a cache of swords and spears hidden beneath their beds. They lived in faith. Faith was indeed their shield.

Now it is interesting, and somewhat inexplicable, that Albert drops a line from Ephesians. Paul tells his readers that their feet should be shod and ready for the Gospel of peace. Albert passes over the question of footwear for his hermits. Perhaps he was anxious to move on to the helmet of salvation, the next item he will mention. It is unlikely that Albert simply overlooked the sentence, he was far too thorough to overlook much. And it would seem that the thought of footwear for the Gospel of peace would have fit in with his overall plan, for the fidelity of the hermits to his *Pattern for Life* would have announced the Gospel of peace to the war-torn land. After all, the project he gave the hermits was a reminder that the enemy was not the flesh and blood enemy camped only a few miles distant from their hermitage, but the ancient enemy of humankind who has sought to destroy us from the beginning. Perhaps Albert did not mention the footwear for bringing the Gospel of peace because he did not wish to give the hermits any justification for the ministry of preaching. It was common for lay hermits, with the permission of the bishop, to preach. Albert may not have wanted to give this permission, but then other sources tell us that the hermits did, at least occasionally, come down from their hermitage to "sow broadcast of the grain they had reaped in contemplation" by preaching.[13] Perhaps Albert wanted them to keep their attention on the battle in which they were engaged and did not want to give them excuse to slacken, to promote a false peace before the land had been won for Christ. In the end, we must simply note

---

[13] This source is a later thirteenth-century Prior General, Nicholas the Frenchman (Nicolas Gallicus) who allegedly wrote the treatise, *The Fiery Arrow* (Ignea Saggita) in which he makes this claim.

that Albert leaves his hermits unshod. This might bring some justification to our discalced brothers and sisters for their lack of footwear.

Paul told the Ephesians that they should take the helmet of salvation and Albert repeats this to the hermits, but adds to it, borrowing from 1 Timothy 1:1 and 4:10 as well as Titus 2:13 and Matthew 1:21 to let us know that Christ is our only Saviour, the one who can set us free from our sins. He also tells the hermits to put the helmet on their heads, even as he had told them to gird their loins and fortify their breasts. In Albert's understanding, clearly derived from and dependent on the various Pauline texts (and texts attributed to Paul), that Christ alone is our hope. Christ alone is our strength. The hermits have been called to a life where Christ is their sole focus. They turn nowhere else for hope of salvation for there is no salvation save in Jesus Christ. Incidentally, this point has recently been reinforced by then-Cardinal Ratzinger when he issued the famous document *Dominus Iesus*. It upset many people, both liberal and conservative, on its insistence that Christ alone is the path to salvation. And too many people understand this as adherence to a formula of doctrine rather than a commitment to a way of living. Faith in Christ is not intellectual assent to doctrine, it is obedience to his Gospel. Albert wanted the hermits to be keenly aware of this need to focus only on Christ and to be faithful in their deeds to him as the only one who could offer them ultimate security. Their hope for winning the land for Christ was not so much in an allegiance to doctrinal orthodoxy, but in their commitment to Christian orthopraxis–Albert doesn't lecture them on doctrine in his *Pattern for Living*, he calls them to live Christ-like lives and spells out a way to do this. All the correct teaching the world does no good whatsoever if Christians do not put their faith into practice. It is not enough that we profess Christ, we must live his way.

Next Albert tells the hermits to take up the Sword of the Spirit, that is the Word of God. Again, he adds to the Pauline text. Borrowing from Colossians 3:1, Deuteronomy 30:14, and Romans 10:8 (all backed up by Job 22:22, Ps 18:15, and Sirach 39:41), Albert wants the hermits to take up the Sword of the Spirit, that is the Word of God, so that Word will take life in their hearts and their mouths. Albert actually uses the phrase *abundanter habitet*, that is "dwell abundantly" to describe what he wants the Word of God to do in their mouths and hearts. And he wants this so that all that they do may be done in the Word of the Lord. Here Albert draws on Colossians 3:17 and, perhaps to a lesser extent, 1 Corinthians 10:31. Their entire lives, all that they say, all that they do, are to be governed by the Word of God.

Now it is important to note that Albert is not only spelling out for them a value system by which they are to live–chastity, meditation, righteousness, faith, etc., but he is also teaching them a methodology for determining their lives, a methodology he makes explicit here in this last phrase. He is teaching them to live the scriptures. They are to base their lives on the scriptures, something which requires them to know the scripture inside and out, and to have prayed the scriptures, examining every detail of their lives in the light of the Word of God. Indeed, his *Pattern for Life* is not a closed book, as it were, which tells them everything they must do. It only gives them a few suggestions. There will be many decisions the hermits will have to make without Albert's guidance. New situations will come up requiring answers and solutions that Albert had never foreseen. But he gives them a methodology. Fill your lives with the Word of God so that everything you do will be done in the Word of God. Perhaps this is his most crucial gift to the hermits, a methodology by which they can discern the will of God in the endlessly unfolding changes of life. They are to be men of the Word of God, disciples who do all in the Word of God.

I think it is important to notice that in all the armour Paul gives the Ephesians, and Albert gives the hermits, there is only one offensive weapon, the Sword of the Spirit, the Word of God. All the other weapons–the armour, the breastplate, the shield–are defensive. God has given us the protection we need in the battle and he authorizes only one weapon–his Word. And his Word is powerful enough to win the world for Christ.

When one studies all the world religions one is impressed by the profundity of beauty and of truth that one can find in each of them. At Vatican II, the decree on non-Christian religions, *Nostra Aetate*, reminds us that all religion contains some truth, some reflection of the truth that God has revealed in its fullness through his Son, Jesus Christ. And at Vatican II, the Church declared that we reject nothing that is true in these religions. Indeed, we rejoice that others have come to a knowledge and even wisdom through what we might call natural revelation of what has been revealed to us supernaturally. Nevertheless, no other religion, for all the good it might contain, can match the stunning revelation that God has given us in Christ Jesus. There is a plan here for the world, a plan that will lead to peace and a just sharing of the plenty which God offers us in creation. If the world believed in Christ, there would be no need for the violence with which some seek to grab what they need and others to protect what they have. But the challenge is for those of us who claim that we believe Christ to be Lord and Saviour–do we live Christian lives? The hermits had to face that fair and square. Were they to be part of the violence of their day or were they to trust the Word of God revealed in Christ Jesus and lead lives of discipleship that required them to love their enemies and pray for their persecutors, to share from their meager stores with those who had less, and to consider all whom they met and even all whom they feared to be the Christ who came in the guise of the hungry, the thirsty, the homeless, the stranger, the naked, the sick, and the imprisoned.

LAY CARMELITES AND THE RULE, CHAPTER 19

If this chapter is so important to Albert's project, we must pay particular attention to it. We too, like the hermits, live in a world of conflict. We must focus on who the true enemy is and not be distracted by claims that our enemy is flesh and blood. Indeed, we must hold no person as our enemy for we know that all people are the sons and daughters of God and that his will is for all to be saved. In the same way, we must not take up any violence against others, but trust that the will of God revealed in Christ Jesus, is sufficient strength for us to defeat the real enemy of humankind, the Evil One who sows the discord among peoples and races and nationalities and religions. We must hold fast to our faith and affirm that while there are things for which we must be willing to die, there is nothing for which God wills that we should kill. As long as we consider any one our enemy, we cannot convincingly call God our Father or Christ our Brother. It is a tremendous challenge, but one which we must embrace if we are to be faithful. We can win the world for Christ, but only by renouncing the world's plan which leads only to war and destruction and suffering. We must not fall for the enemy's lies.

We must first of all gird ourselves in chastity. Now this is chastity according to our state of life. For married people, that is chastity within marriage. It means not only fidelity but using the gift of human sexuality according to the divine plan. This subject has already been discussed under the promise or vow of chastity in chapter 4 of the Rule, but this provides us with an opportunity to comment further and to reinforce the idea of marital chastity as a sacred use of the gift of human sexuality. We Christians, at least we orthodox Christians, hold marital sexuality in high regard. Unfortunately, the understanding of human sexuality has for many Christians been tainted by several heresies–Gnosticism and Manicheanism in the third and fourth centuries and Jansenism in the seventeenth century and continuing until the present. Some have come to see marital sexuality not as Saint Paul presents it, as the sacramental expression of the love of Christ and his Church, but rather as a concession to human weakness for those who are not strong enough for celibacy. In the sacrament of marriage a man and a woman have the opportunity to give of themselves to one another in love, to surrender themselves not to their own desire, but to the fulfillment and happiness of the spouse. This is a sacred responsibility. It is a witness to the world of the power of love to empty us of our own selfishness and allow us to live for others. No human love is more perfect than the love of a Christian husband for his wife, of a Christian wife for her husband. But this love is not arrived at through natural means. Like all virtue it is dependent on grace but also requires training and practice. It is something that the husband and wife must grow in through the years of their marriage.

I have had married Lay Carmelites tell me that they practice celibacy in their marriages. They expect me to be impressed, in fact I am scandalized. In the first place, virtue–were this to be a virtue and not a vice–should always be practiced in discreet silence. Such a decision should be a matter which is discussed only their spiritual director and confessor. The very ease with which they talk about it would cheapen the virtue, again were it a virtue. But what is particularly sad about it is that these people do not understand the vocation to which God has called them in the sacrament of matrimony. Here they are called to witness to the unitive love between Christ and his Church, between the soul and God, and they leave the gift untouched.

There is a sense in which the lovemaking between a husband and wife parallels the privilege of the priest in saying Mass for the Church. The sacrament of marriage does not begin and end with lovemaking, and the sacrament of Holy Orders does not begin and end with the celebration of the Eucharistic sacrifice. But the husband and wife are never more husband and wife, than when they become one flesh in the act of lovemaking, and the priest is never more a priest than when he stands at the altar as the visible representation of Christ the Priest who gave his life for his Church in the Eucharist. It is sad, tragically sad, when priests don't make themselves available to the Church when it is hungry for the Body and Blood of the Lord. It is equally sad when a husband or a wife close themselves off to their spouse when the spouse is seeking an opportunity to express the deep and passionate love to which the grace of the sacrament of matrimony has called them. Chaste love in marriage is about surrender of self to another. Lay Carmelites who are married must cultivate a deep and spiritual appreciation for the gift of human sexuality which God entrusted to them on their wedding day.

Of course, for those who are not married, the sanctity of human sexuality requires that we not mimic the sacred use of sexuality between husband and wife by any activity that would use our sexual gifts outside the bonds of matrimony. In this way we too, whether Religious or single, testify to the sacredness of the gift of human sexuality. We are like the friend of the bridegroom who waits outside the door of the wedding chamber that Jesus speaks of in John 3:29. We rejoice in the sexual intimacy of the married and honor that intimacy by not counterfeiting it with less noble relationships. The chastity of the unmarried testifies to the sacredness of chaste marital sexuality.

In the second place we are called to fortify ourselves with holy meditations. This is very important for us Carmelites for our lives should be constant meditation, day and night, on the Law, that is the Word, of the Lord. We need to surrender ourselves to the Word and reflect on it at every opportunity. To do this we should give ourselves over to some spiritual reading with regularity. This does not mean that we can have no interest other than "spiritual things." That would make us bad advertisements for Carmel, much less for faith in Christ. No, we should be able to bring our whole and varied lives to prayer as we reflect on the mystery of life in the light of Christ and his word. We can bring a ball game to our prayerful reflection as well as a charitable deed, a popular song as well as a hymn. God speaks to us in all the events of our day; we can learn to listen to him in all the events and in each of the people, who make up our lives. Indeed we must stop dividing God's creation into spheres that are "sacred" and spheres that are "secular." Rather we must learn to see that all creation mirrors the glory of God. We are called to integrate the various aspects of human life and bring them together in the light of the Gospel of Christ. This is true holiness, authentic spirituality.

When we are called to put on the breastplate of righteousness, it is precisely this integration that is required. To be right with God means that our whole lives have to be subjected to his authority. Our employment, our hobbies, our family life, our reading, our household chores, our hobbies and interests, our entertainment–it all must come together in Christ. Our entire life must stand with integrity before God. How we spend our money, how we spend our time, how we vote, the friends we associate with must all stand within the plan of God. Again, this does not mean that we have to withdraw from ordinary life, but rather that we bring our lives to Christ and we bring Christ into our lives. We don't have to talk about Jesus, in fact better that we witness by our deeds than our words, but we must strive to be people who are upright and honest, compassionate and understanding, of sound values ourselves without judging others. And the bottom line of all this is we must be men and women who are known for loving God and for loving our neighbor. We must strive to be the sort of person about whom others say–he is so generous, she is so compassionate, she is always there for you when you need a friend, he is the sort of friend you want to have when life is treating you badly. Saint John of the Cross says that in the evening of our lives we will be judged by our love. We must be men and women who will not be found lacking in love. And remember, love is not a feeling; it is the acts of a will that is set on the good, spiritual and temporal, of others. All the feeling in the world won't budge the gates of heaven one bit, but a single surrender of our will to achieve the good of another can bring down the gates of hell.

When we speak of the breastplate of righteousness or justice, we must remember that we have no justice of our own. In the sight of God we each would be only a sinner had not Christ given us of his justice and clothed us in his righteousness. It is, after all, his holiness that distinguishes us and certainly not our own. This is important because it prevents us from taking pride in our own worthiness, and it embarrasses us into showing mercy, not judgment, to others in their failings. The armour, after all, is not ours, it is God's. Any justice or holiness or righteousness of our own would be pathetic protection against the snares of the Evil One. But when we are clothed in the righteousness of Christ, when we are transformed into Christ, we cannot but love God with all our heart, soul, and strength, and we cannot but love our neighbor as ourselves.

And then there is the shield of faith. Faith too is not a feeling, but a commitment of the will to act consistently with the will of God. In the English-speaking world we have too long laid emphasis on the *feelings* that one has, but feelings are one of the most dangerous tools of self-deception. This is not to say that feelings are bad, they are not. But we must be very honest and ask ourselves if there is more to our faith–and our love–than our feelings. In periods of spiritual dryness, and above all in the dark nights of the senses and of the spirit, we may be utterly bereft of spiritual feelings, or worse, we may have feelings of doubt and insecurity. That does not mean we have lost our faith. The measure of faith is obedience to the will of God even as the only sure measure of love of God is the love we have for our neighbor.

The confusion of certain religious feelings for faith is rooted in Protestant piety, especially coming out of the Methodist movement. John Wesley, the Anglican priest who founded Methodism, had a life-long desire to *feel* saved in his faith. Wesley was a very competent theologian, as well as a profoundly holy man, and he knew that faith was more than this feeling, but his obsession with this issue of feeling led many of his disciples to over-value the feelings that accompany the early stages of the spiritual life. This has spread in the English-speaking world to many Catholics. They do not realize that *feelings* of spiritual intimacy are markers of only the earliest stages of the spiritual life. Because they *feel* deeply their faith they think they have arrived at a depth of faith, when in fact the feelings testify to their spiritual immaturity. They have not yet been tried by the dark nights where we learn to value our feelings for what they are–the consolation and encouragement of the weak soul to grow in faith through the trials ahead. The best guarantee of our faith is not our feelings, but our actions. Faith will bear a harvest of good works. Good works, without faith, have no value in the sight of God and they cannot bring us any justification with God. But faith, authentic faith, will always bear a harvest of good works, of charity. Faith without works is dead, despite whatever feelings we may have. Strive to live your faith, not feel it.

On the other hand, for too many Catholics–especially those of a certain age or too far over on the right-wing of the Church, faith is often reduced to no more than subscribing to a certain perceived orthodoxy. A person has faith if they intellectually agree to certain doctrines. While it is important for us to subscribe to the faith of the Church, that is, to the doctrines which the Church teaches for salvation, we cannot confuse intellectual assent with faith. Again, the proof is in the pudding and our faith can be ascertained only by our conformity to the divine will. In the end, if we were to fail an exam in dogma we can still be saved. The victory, after all, lies not in our knowledge but in our faith. The question is not what we believe, but Who we believe. Faith is not a matter of conforming our intellect, but our wills. Believe what the Church teaches and move on to putting your trust in Christ by taking his Gospel and making it the plan of your life. Ultimately people will come to Christ not because of all the glorious doctrines and splendid rituals of the Church but because of the glorious grace and splendid holiness our lives in Christ manifest.

Next Albert tells us to take up the helmet of salvation and set it firmly on our heads. Put on the Lord Jesus Christ–the Apostle Paul tells us in Romans–and make no provisions for the desires of the flesh. We must put on Christ–become Christ, be transformed into Christ. It is no longer I who live, Paul tells the Galatians, it is Christ Jesus who lives in me. Christ himself is the helmet of salvation and in putting on Christ we are delivered from out sins–not merely that our sins are forgiven, but as we are transformed into Christ, sin looses its power over us. Actually Paul's quote to the Galatians reads: I have been crucified with Christ, it is no longer I who live but Christ Jesus who lives in me. This corresponds to Paul's letter to the Romans where he says

"Shall we persist in sin that grace may abound? Of Course not! How can we who died to sin yet live in it? Are you not aware that we who were baptized into Christ Jesus were baptized into his death? We were indeed buried with him through baptism into death, so that, just as Christ was raised from the dead by the Glory of the Father, we too might live in newness of life. (Romans 6:1-4)"

When we put on Christ we are set free, not just from our sins, but set free from sin itself. This is not an instantaneous thing of course, we mature in Christ. The transformation is a slow and gradual one, taking the span of our lives, but as we mature in Christ all else but Christ slowly looses its hold on us. And there is no greater aid in this than frequent participation in the Holy Eucharist for we truly become not what we eat, but whom we eat. We offer to the Father not bread and wine for he has no need of bread and wine. We offer our lives–our work, our energy, our dreams, our very being. And it is we, not merely the bread and wine, who are transformed into Christ. We devour Christ and he slowly but surely devours us into himself.

Incidentally, for us Carmelites, the scapular is an outward sign (sacramental) of this determination to put on Christ. The prayer in imposing the scapular on Carmelite Religious when they receive the habit has always told us to "take up the yoke of Christ for his yoke is easy and his burden light." Putting on the yoke of Christ is a visible symbol of conforming to his teachings in our lives. We are, of course, called to much more than conforming to his teaching. We are called to conform ourselves to him totally so that our will becomes one with his will which is one with the will of the Father. "If any one would be my disciple, let him take up his cross and follow me." As we put on our scapulars we should remind ourselves that our vocation is to live totally in Christ.

Albert also reminds us Christ is our only Saviour. We can look nowhere else for salvation. Even the graces which come through the intercession of the Blessed Virgin come from Christ for there is no salvation other than that which Christ has won for us. Christ is the total focus of our lives. Our spirituality is totally Christocentric. We give due homage to the Blessed Virgin and to the saints, but our only hope is in Christ. Like Mary herself, we never take our eyes off Christ. There is no other Name in which we hope for salvation. Consequently our lives revolves around his Word in the Scriptures, especially the Gospel, his sacrifice at Calvary made present in the Mass, his flesh and blood present in the Eucharist, and his Body which is the Church. The Real and True Presence of Christ is not limited to the Eucharist and we seek to live in his Presence continually by living in his Word and by strengthening the bonds of Communion in his Body the Church. And we remember too that although he is hidden from our eyes, it is he who is present in the hungry, the thirsty, the naked, the stranger, the sick, the imprisoned and in all the least of his brothers and sisters. Indeed, as we grow in conformity to him we come to realize he is always at our elbow, never even a step away from us, hidden from view but available to the touch.

This brings us to the final point of this chapter. Again, seeking to live in constant communion with Christ, we desire that his Word be constantly in our hearts (in meditation) and on our lips (in prayer) that all that we do we might do in his Word. And this Word, to which we strive to be always present, is indeed the Sword of the Spirit. It is the heaven-sent weapon by which we can win the world for Christ. When all the might of nations fails to bring peace but causes only war and division and suffering, the Word of God offers us hope. If we take God at his Word, take his Word seriously and attempt to live it in every detail, we shall be mighty warriors for God bringing about the Kingdom of Peace which Christ proclaims. But this means that the Word must be our only weapon. We cannot resort to violence or assent to violence of any kind if we are to put our trust in the Sword of the Spirit, that is the Word of God. We must gamble entirely on that Word. If we are to live by faith, we cannot hedge our bets. Too many Christians try to keep a foot in both camps–the camp of earthly might and the camp of God's Protection. We must make a choice, the choice of God and his promise, for protection. This is one of the hardest decisions we must make in life. The Prophets told the ancient Israelites to put their trust in God, not in the earthly alliances of armies and kings. When they put their trust in God, they found security. When they put their trust in princes, they lost it all. So too we must be confident that living the Gospel will be strength enough to prevail over any obstacle. This is not a promise that it will be easy, but rather that in the end God will triumph. Choosing the Word of God to be our only strength will set us apart from most people who lack the courage to trust God and will want guarantees of political or military power for their safety. In the short run their course may seem the more prudent. But history has clearly demonstrated that peace and justice never come about by violence. The path of the Gospel is yet to be tried. We must be pioneers in this choice. As Chesterton said: it is not that Christianity has been tried and found wanting, it is that it has been found difficult and left untried.

And so this is the path of spiritual warfare that the Carmelite today, like the hermit of old, must dedicate himself or herself too. We too live on the frontier, the enemy is camped not far away. But the enemy is not flesh and blood, but the eternal Enemy of God and his chosen ones. Stand firm in the Gospel and we will win the world for Christ, overcoming violence and hatred by the power of his Word. The battle is ours and we will prevail if we put on the armour of God and stand firm in the fight.

Chapter 20

Albert

You must give yourselves to work of some kind, so that the devil may always find you busy; no idleness on your part must give him a chance to pierce the defences of your souls. In this respect you have both the teaching and the example of Saint Paul the Apostle, into whose mouth Christ put his own words. God made him preacher and teacher of faith and truth to the nations: with him as your leader you cannot go astray. We lived among you, he said, labouring and wary, toiling night and day so as not to be a burden to any of you; not because we had no power to do otherwise but so as to give you, in your own selves, an example you might imitate. For the charge we gave you when we were with you was this: that whoever is not willing to work should not be allowed to eat either. For we have heard that there are certain restless idlers among you. We charge people of this kind, and implore them in the name of our Lord Jesus Christ, that they earn their own bread by silent toil.

Pope Innocent IV (the 1247 revision)
You must give yourselves to work of some kind, so that the devil may always find you busy; no idleness on your part must give him a chance to pierce the defences of your souls. In this respect you have both the teaching and the example of Saint Paul the Apostle, into whose mouth Christ put his own words. God made him preacher and teacher of faith and truth to the nations: with him as your leader you

cannot go astray. We lived among you, he said, labouring and wary, toiling night and day so as not to be a burden to any of you; not because we had no power to do otherwise but so as to give you, in your own selves, an example you might imitate. For the charge we gave you when we were with you was this: that whoever is not willing to work should not be allowed to eat either. For we have heard that there are certain restless idlers among you. We charge people of this kind, and implore them in the name of our Lord Jesus Christ, that they earn their own bread by silent toil. This is the way of holiness and goodness: see that you follow it.

Lay hermits customarily supported themselves by manual labour and by alms. It was against their vocational call, "naked to follow the naked Christ," to live off fixed incomes or from the work of others except given as charity. The hermits then would almost certainly have included some reference to work in their proposal to Albert, though if they did so he did not merely embroider it with some scripture references, as he did the mandate to remain in or near their cells or the section on holding property in common, but removed it and rewrote it entirely, inserting it into the chapters that he seems to have added to their original proposal. For all practical purposes then this chapter is part of his contribution and should not be seen as part of their proposal. The heart of this chapter is almost a direct quote from 2 Thessalonians 3:7-12. It is the longest scriptural citation in the Rule and it is published without comment as Albert saw that it was totally self-explanatory. He sets it like a jewel in a setting fashioned from other scriptural references such as 2 Corinthians 13:3, less explicitly in 2 Corinthians 2:17 and 12:19, and 1 Timothy 2:7.

Although this passage is, in one respect, vintage Albert for its style of biblical reference, it actually can be found, at least substantively, not only in a variety of Rules but throughout the vast corpus of monastic literature. In fact, Augustine, in his Rule, cites the same passage of Second Thessalonians in his exhortation to work and it subsequently becomes standard in Religious Rules. It also mirrors the teaching of the great fifth-century monastic author, John Cassian, whose works were read in every monastic refectory in Europe for a thousand years and whose wisdom seeped its way out of the monasteries and into the mainstream of western spirituality.

Innocent's revisers, picking up on Albert's technique, added the final sentence in 1247 "This is the way of holiness and goodness: see that you follow it," borrowed from Isaiah 30:21; Jeremiah 6:16 and, to a lesser extent dependent on 1 Kings 8:36 and Proverbs 2:20.

Lay Carmelites and the Rule, Chapter 20.

This chapter is a clear instruction on the importance of work to any one who follows the Carmelite way of life. We work not just to support ourselves–there are, after all, some Lay Carmelites whose financial situation does not require them to work–but because work is an important and essential part of the spiritual diet. Our being good stewards, not only of our finances, but of our time and our talents demands that we use our time and talents to further the kingdom of God. Our vocation to live simply would direct us that even if we are fiscally able to employ others to take care of some of the routine tasks of life–the gardening, the preparation of meals, the laundry or housework–that we ourselves do as much as we are able and depend as little as possible on the work of others. Servants are an embarrassment to those who themselves are called by the Master to service. And when it is necessary, because of age, or health, or other more pressing commitments (such as our own employment, or charitable work outside the home) to employ others in service roles, we never treat them as servants but as collaborators. We certainly do not employ others so that we can be people of leisure. We see the tasks that need to be done before the Master returns and we dedicate ourselves to that work. We are, after all, all servants.

To the extent that our time is free we use it in the service of others. There is tremendous need in our world. There are sick who need care, sorrowful who need consolation, youth who need guidance. The homeless have their needs. Young mothers have needs. There is much to do to help at the church or the Catholic school. Agencies that help women choose life for their unborn children can use our help. In addition many Lay Carmelites have particular talents–sewing, painting, music, baking–that can be put at the service of the Church or of people in need. Our homes should be places of hospitable welcome to all who come there, and hospitality itself requires work.

Most Lay Carmelites have a financial need to work to support themselves and their families. Sometimes the demands of our work preclude our doing much more than that for which we are paid a salary. We might like to help at the parish or be active in a local charity but, in all honesty do not have the time left over in the day to do so. We should never be embarrassed by this. It may not be poverty but it does mirror the life at Nazareth where the carpenter father and his carpenter son undoubtedly worked long and hard. But even in our secular employment we should see that the work of God is being done. We must come to our work in a way that gives our employer his due work in return for our salaries. We must come to our work in a way that witnesses to our co-workers our sense of charity towards them and justice to our employer as well as pride in what we do. We need to take pride in our work, doing the best that we are able. And, of course, we must behave like Christian men and women in every respect. Christians look at work as a dignity and an honour. In our work we collaborate in some small way with the creative work of God in the world. We must keep in mind, however, that people are always more important than things, including work. Work sustains us materially, but relationships are the purpose for which God has created us. Our relationship with God is foundational, but it must bloom into love for our neighbour if God's will is to be done.

Chapter 21

Albert

The apostle would have us keep silence, for in silence he tells us to work. As the Prophet also makes known to us: Silence is the way to foster holiness. Elsewhere he says: Your strength will lie in silence and hope. For this reason I lay down that you are to keep silence from Vespers until Terce the next day, unless some necessary or good reason, or the prior's permission, should break the silence. At other times although you need not keep silence so strictly, be careful not to indulge in a great deal of talk, for as Scripture has it–and experience teaches us no less–sin will not be wanting where there is much talk and whoever is careless in speech will come to harm; and elsewhere; the use of many words brings harm to the speaker's soul. And our Lord says in the Gospel: Every vain word uttered will have to be accounted for on judgment day. Make a balance then, each of you, to weigh your words in; keep a tight rein on your mouths, lest you should stumble and fall in speech, and your fall be irreparable and prove mortal. Like the Prophet, watch your step lest your tongue give offense, and employ every care in keeping silent, which is the way to foster holiness.

Pope Innocent IV (the 1247 revision)
The Apostle would have us keep silence, for in silence he tells us to work. As the Prophet also makes known to us: Silence is the way to foster holiness. Elsewhere he says: Your strength will lie in silence

and hope. For this reason I lay down that you are to keep silence from after Compline until after Prime the next day. At other times, although you need not keep silence so strictly, be careful not to indulge in a great deal of talk, for, as Scripture has it – and experience teaches us no less – sin will not be wanting where there is much talk, and he who is careless in speech will come to harm; and elsewhere: The use of many words brings harm to the speaker's soul. And our Lord says in the Gospel: Every rash word uttered will have to be accounted for on judgement day. Make a balance then, each of you, to weigh his words in; keep a tight rein on your mouths, lest you should stumble and fall in speech, and your fall be irreparable and prove mortal. Like the Prophet, watch your step lest your tongue give offence, and employ every care in keeping silent, which is the way to foster holiness.

In writing to the Thessalonians about work, Paul mentions to them that they should work in silence. It is not his major point, but Albert seizes on it to introduce a chapter about silence. Silence is a key virtue in the spiritual life. We cannot hear God speak unless we learn the silence that permits his voice to be heard. In our Carmelite tradition, we look to the experience of Elijah at Horeb (1 Kings 19: 1-14) and listen for God in the silence. In fact, silence was an essential part of the monastic discipline as well. It was absolutely essential in traditional monasteries with their great refectories and common dormitories where the community spent so much of the day–and night–together. Silence was a key element to how a monk in a large community achieved psychological solitude in a system that allowed little or no physical solitude. Monastic silence was of two types–the ordinary silence of the day in which necessary communication was permitted, and the grand silence of the night in which there was absolutely no communication whatsoever between monks. Albert borrows this distinction and imposes the heavier silence from Vespers (late afternoon) until Terce (about two hours after sun-up) the next morning. During the remainder of the day the hermits were adjured to avoid superfluous speech but permitted to talk. Albert also permitted the hermits some leeway during the night silence. Good reason, or the permission of the prior, allowed for the night silence to be broken. When one is familiar with the rigid monastic "grand silence" this is actually a very generous leeway.

When Innocent revised the Rule he shortened the silence but he also did away with the leeway for the night silence. The night silence began after Compline–the final liturgical prayer of the day, said in the mid-evening, until prime, about sun-up the next morning. The reason he did away with the leeway is that increasingly the Carmelites were not living in individual hermitages, but in more traditional conventual buildings, monastic style buildings. The little hermit cells, each a house to itself with some distance from the neighbour, were increasingly being replaced with individual rooms along common corridors. This was probably meant to be a temporary arrangement at the beginning–until the resources were there to build hermitages–but it soon became the norm.[14] In a her-

---

[14] See Nicholas Gallicus and *The Fiery Arrow* on this point.

mitage, a conversation could be carried on without disturbing one's neighbours. In a small room in a dormitory corridor, sound would travel more easily and disturb others. The reason for shortening the silence was that increasingly the Carmelites were living not in rural settings, but in or near the towns. Their life was not as secluded and their day most likely did not wind down as early. There might still be people to see in the late afternoon, business that had to be taken care of, errands that needed to be run. The same would be true in the early morning. In the medieval world, the business day in the town started early. People might be joining them in church for Mass in the morning or vespers in the evening. Their common supper, at least on days when there was no fast, would not be until after Vespers and while they listened to scripture during the meal, some conversation before or after would be normal. While the decrease in solitude should have made silence all the more appreciated, it in fact created an inconvenience and Innocent simply shortened its period.

But Innocent did not take away the principle. He knew that too much talking was unhealthy, an occasions for frivolous conversation, gossip, backbiting and worse. He kept Albert's admonition to keep talk to a minimum and give serious consideration whether something needed to be said before saying it.

Lay Carmelites and the Rule, Chapter 21

We too need to give serious thought to our conversation. In fact, a very good form of fasting is to give up use of the telephone, or at least its non-essential use, for a designated period of time. And silence requires not only that we keep out mouth shut, but that we turn off the television, the radio, our walkmans and ipods, and now, the internet. We claim that some religious music helps us pray, and that can be true at the early stages of prayer, but as we mature in the spiritual life we find even religious music a distraction. Turn it off. Learn to be in silence. Too many people today turn on the television as soon as they come in the house; some even have multiple televisions going. "I don't listen to them," they say, "I just like the sound of some voices when I am in the house by myself." Learn to prefer the sound of silence. We can make good use of our time in the car listening to various Public Radio shows, religious programming, or books on tape. We can make better use of our time alone in the car learning to cultivate silence.

Never use silence, however, as an escape from charity. No matter how much we appreciate the luxury of solitude and silence–and once we learn them they do become a luxurious pleasure–charity always demands that we put them aside to tend to the needs of others. In a similar way, never use silence or solitude as a means of showing off your spiritual life. As with fasting, learn to be inconspicuous and your Father in heaven who sees what is done inconspicuously, will reward you. In family life, it would be very impractical and even rude to try to keep some sort of night silence. Silence in the night is not only for ourselves but for the benefit of others, so that they can rest or pray, and when it benefits them–letting them sleep restfully–honour it, but when your spouse, or a family member, or a guest wants company and conversation, give it to them. More is always gained by giving up our own pleasure, however spiritual, than by denying another his or her rightful happiness.

Of course, sometimes it is a wonderful luxury in the night to come down from our room and sit alone in a chair in the dark and just listen to the silence and to the One who speaks in the silence. Or perhaps we find a pleasure in coming downstairs early in the morning and wrapping ourselves in a blanket and drinking our coffee as we pray the Liturgy of the Hours or do our spiritual reading. Carve out what silent moments you can, even if it means getting in the car, driving around the corner and parking for a half hour while you pray Evening Prayer. Find the times and places where you can be alone and enjoy the gift of silence.

Chapter 22

You, brother B., and whoever may succeed you as prior, must always keep in mind and put into practice what our Lord said in the Gospel: Whoever has a mind to become a leader among you must make himself servant to the rest, and whichever of you would be first must become your bondsman.

Here Albert begins to bring his letter and the *Formula Vitae* to a close. Kees Waaijman says that this paragraph and the succeeding are the *petitio* of the letter. Albert is directly asking something, first of the prior, later of the hermits. The prior is to remember–and put into practice–Our Lord's command that whoever is first must be servant of the others. Authority is given not to rule or have power, but to serve.

LAY CARMELITES AND THE RULE, CHAPTER 22

The President of the Community, or the Prior, or whatever the leader is called, must keep in mind that his or her role is one of service to the others. This means not only service to the community as a whole, but to each of its members. The role of the leader is to make life richer for the others. Being the president or the prior is not a position that brings any power with it. The disciple of Christ must always eschew power. Authority, the ability to inspire others to follow, is a charism. Power, the strength to compel others to follow, is for Christians a vice.

The leader must always help the community to discern the call that the Spirit is giving to the community. The vision, in the Carmelite tradition, is not given to the leader, it is given to the community. A good leader does not tell the community what to do or where they must go, but helps the community to listen to the grace being given the community itself. To often bad leadership either breaks the community apart or makes it dependent on the leader for guidance. The need of the leader for his or her ego to be massaged by complacent followers leaves a community and its members bereft of the ability to discern the call of

God that comes through a spiritually mature community itself. This can be as much a problem for the Religious of the Order as for the Lay Communities. Some people have a compulsive need to be in control. They are convinced that no one else can lead the community at this time as well as they. Sometimes they are right, or would be right, if the instinct were not proceeding from a compulsive need. A community must remember that however talented a leader is, if they have a *need* to be the leader, they are the wrong person. Similarly, some people have excellent ideas or wonderful vision for the community, but they cannot exercise leadership in a way that allows the ideas and vision of the others to come to the fore. Things must be done their way, according to their plan. They, no matter how talented they are, should not be chosen for leadership until they learn how to set aside their own agenda and trust the vision of the community.

One of the signs of bad leadership is that it isn't able to let go of its control when the time comes for a change of leadership. In Carmel we do not elect our leaders for life, but for fixed terms. There is normally a term-limit on the leadership as well. Sometimes needy people get around this term-limit by standing aside for a term while a trusted subordinate fills the office and is little more than a puppet, a willing puppet perhaps, but a puppet. We see this among the Religious at times as well as the Lay Carmelites. Stability in leadership–the same faces on the Council term after term–is usually a danger sign. Husbands and wives succeeding one another, or worse, alternating with one another, is usually a danger sign. A person serving two terms and then being out for one or two and then back in is usually a danger sign. A person who has been either a leader or a councilor consistently for ten years or longer is usually a danger sign. The operative word here is "usually," there are exceptions to every rule, but if the community is healthy and has been empowered by good leadership that trusts the community and its vision, there will be many people who can serve in positions of leadership. Because the vision belongs to the community and not to the individual, anyone who can facilitate the community's discernment process can lead. Anyone who is a good listener, who can guide a frank and open discussion, and is not wed to their own ideas can help the community chart its course and can make the necessary day by day decisions that stay within that common vision. This is a much more difficult leadership style, however, than those who just take control and plough ahead as they see best. That is why one sign of a good leader is the willingness to step down and let others have their turn.

CHAPTER 23

You, other brothers too, hold your prior in humble reverence, your minds not on him but on Christ who has placed him over you, and who, to those who rule the Churches, addressed the words: Whoever pays you heed pays heed to me, and whoever treats you with dishonour dishonours me; if you remain so minded you will not be found guilty of contempt, but will merit life eternal as fit reward for your obedience.

This is the second part of the *petitio*. As the prior must remember that he is called to be servant of the community, so the brothers, or sisters, must hold their prior in humble reverence. They must see beyond the limitations of the individual and see Christ from whom the leader draws his authority because, like Christ, he is servant. In the Benedictine tradition, the abbot stands in the place of Christ, in the Person of Christ. The abbot becomes Christ in the community. Albert is not saying precisely that, his vision of the leader is a more humble one, but he is saying that Christ has established the leader in his role of leadership. This binds the leader, of course, to the servant role that Christ has established, but once the leader has accepted that role of servant to the community, then the community must honour the leader and listen to him. This means, of course, that the authority the leader is able to exercise will be directly proportionate to how well he listens to Christ's admonition to be servant to the others. Just as service is the path to salvation for the prior, obedience and reverence is the path of salvation for the other brothers or sisters.

LAY CARMELITES AND THE RULE, CHAPTER 23

Lay Carmelites must work with the leader the community has chosen. This can be very difficult, especially when we ourselves may have been hoping to be chosen and were overlooked in favour of another. Often communities split after an election, or suffer the loss of several members, which only shows the bad faith of those who cannot accept the new leadership. When we understand leadership as service having someone chosen whom we do not like is not a problem. When leadership is about our egos, it can be a huge problem. But the more conformed we are to Christ in his humility the more we can accept the leadership of our peers, even those who are less gifted than we are. When our leaders remember that they model to us Christ the servant of his brothers and sisters, it becomes a pleasure to cooperate with them in the work of the community. Saint Teresa of Avila was once elected prioress of a monastery in which many of the nuns did not want her leadership. They even tried to barricade her out. But when she came into office she won all the sisters over by her humble service to them. My experience is that most of the time when there is a problem with the leadership of the community it is either because the leadership has forgotten their role is to serve or because one or more in the community want to be leaders, not to serve their brothers or sisters, but to "take charge" and make the community into something that they, not necessarily the community, want it to be. It is important that each of us let go of any personal ambition that we have to hold positions of leadership, even when we believe that we can be better leaders than we currently have. Personal ambition, even when it is for the good, becomes a poison in the soul. Let us become ambitious instead for others, always looking at others and seeing who would be good leaders, who has the gifts our community needs. And rather than seek positions for ourselves, let us pray for our leadership, that they are open to the graces God gives them to serve the community well.

CHAPTER 24

Here then are the few points I have written down to provide you with a standard of conduct to live up to; but our Lord, at his second coming will reward anyone who does more than he is obliged to do. See that the bounds of common sense are not exceeded, however, for common sense is the guide of the virtues.

Albert brings his *Pattern for Life* to a close, admitting that it is a simple way, a beginning as it were in the life of discipleship. It is not a long Rule like Benedict, nor a very specific one in its detail like some other Rules. Many issues are not addressed. There is no mention of a habit, for example. The details of fasting are not spelled out. Penances are not assigned for various infractions. Rights and privileges are left unnumbered. While there is a profound spirituality, and a monastic spirituality in the sense of the desert monks of old, there is no sense of a monastic discipline. Most important, however, is that the Rule is open-ended. It is not exhaustive. It gives the basics, but here Albert encourages the hermits to use his *Pattern for Life* as a springboard. With a somewhat veiled allusion to the parable of the Good Samaritan, he tells them that the Lord as his return, much like the Samaritan on his return to the innkeeper, will reward whatever extra effort and expense we have gone to in order to serve him. The Lord will not be outdone in his generosity. Albert closes with the wise words that moderate that enthusiasm, however. Drawing from John Cassian, he insists that the hermits are to see that "the bounds of common sense are not exceeded... for common sense is the guide of the virtues." While the point can be made that ordinarily "common sense" is not the most literal translation of the Latin word *discretio*, it serves well here to put a check on well-meaning but extreme religious practices that in the big picture do little good and sometimes much harm.

LAY CARMELITES AND THE RULE, CHAPTER 24.

Perhaps this is this chapter that most clearly tells us that Albert's *Pattern for Life* is suited not only for Religious but to anyone. Albert admits that it is not some fancy Rule that regulates every detail of life, but a few simple points that provide a foundation for a life of discipleship. It obliges little and encourages much. It leaves open the way for multiple possibilities of adaptation to different situations of life and even vocations in the Church. That is why English Friars and American Hermits and Spanish Nuns and Indonesian Sisters and, yes Carmelite Laity of many nationalities and cultures, can find in it a way of life that guides them in their allegiance to Jesus Christ. Carmelites come in all sorts of variations–behind grilles, in the classroom, flying airplanes, performing surgery, gardening, visiting the sick, directing research projects, wearing habits, not wearing habits, and even in bed with their wives. There are Carmelites in Viet Nam, the Turkana desert of Kenya, behind a grille in Lisieux, in a restaurant kitchen in Rome, in the Andes mountains of Peru and Bolivia, on rafts on the Amazon, in Toyotas in the South Side of Chicago and North Side of London, and, at any given moment, in God-alone-knows how many airport boarding areas. The first Carmelites in Kenya were the Third Order. The Donum Dei Missionary Family has been responsible for bringing their Carmelite brothers to a number of countries. When the Order was suppressed in Portugal and Spain in the nineteenth century, it was the Third Order that kept Carmel alive until the Friars and Nuns could return. And somehow or other, directly or indirectly, all these women and men who make up the Carmelite family can find guidance in the same 1108 Latin words that make up this ancient document.

What might be best stressed, however, is the very final admonition, to let common sense be the guide of how we choose to adapt this *Pattern for Life* to our lives. At times we all, Religious as well as Laity, loose our sense of perspective and become, at the least idiosyncratic (and at the worse absolutely wacky), in our attempts to please God. The only thing that pleases God, of course, is that we become more like him, that is that our true nature, which like his is love, is allowed to shine through the fractured clay pots of our lives. The Laity in following Albert's *Pattern for Life* must not try to become Religious. That is not their vocation. When the Laity want to confine themselves to their homes or live as hermits-in-the-world they are appropriating a vocation that is not theirs. It is a bit affected, if not actually tinged with some sort of spiritual conceit, to mimic the vocation of the Nuns or the Religious Hermits. One can maintain the contemplative discipline appropriate to Carmel without some sort of conspicuous *faux*-cloister. The same would apply to affecting some sort of a religious habit. One can dress simply without drawing some sort of attention to oneself. We should avoid extravagant displays of public piety as well and for the same reason, they draw attention to us. Our mannerisms in church, or in any public place, should conform to the standard etiquette that is expected. In the manner of receiving Holy Communion, for example, we follow the guidelines of the local church. Where they kneel, we kneel. Where they stand, we stand. We simply don't make an issue of these things. God is not glorified in our extravagances, even our extravagances of worship. He is glorified in the lavishness of our charity performed generously but without others seeing us. Indeed, for those who follow the Rule of Saint Albert the scriptures themselves are our guide in the spiritual life. We give the devotional fancies of the current movements a pass and pray discreetly as we always have, seeking to be hidden in the Presence of God while living in the world in which he has placed us.

Some closing considerations
The Role of Scripture in the Rule

One of the most interesting aspects of the Rule is the role that scripture plays in it. Albert quotes scripture, paraphrases scripture, alludes to scripture, cuts and pastes scriptural references together in new ways, and juxtaposes scriptural references in ways that bring out new meanings. The amazing thing is just how much scripture he uses. And, as Craig Morrison has demonstrated in his research, Albert actually draws on two different Latin texts of the bible, Saint Jerome's *Vulgate* and the older *Vetus Latina*. In addition to scripture, Albert also draws on the wisdom of various patristic authors, especially those in the monastic tradition, and above all John Cassian.

In using scripture as he does, Albert roots his vision for a life of discipleship, of *obsequio Ihesu Christi*, in the Word of God. This not only gives an impeccable authority to his vision, but he shows the hermits how they can resolve issues that his *Pattern for Life* may not have foreseen. No one, not even a wise Patriarch like Albert, could foresee every situation that would arise. When confronted with the need to make a decision that Albert's text had not prepared them for, the hermits must simply turn prayerfully and attentively to the Word of God as their source of inspiration. This would be true not only for the community, but for individuals as well. Albert lays out a spirituality that is thoroughly saturated in the Word of God. The hermits are told to meditate day and night on the Law of the Lord. They are told to pray the psalms throughout the day in their cells. They are told to take up the Sword of the Spirit, that is the Word of God, so that all that they might do they might do with the Word of the Lord for accompaniment. When one becomes so drenched in the Word of God the scriptures become our basic vocabulary. We begin not only to express ourselves in the words of scripture, but to even structure our perception of reality according to that Word. The scriptures become our life-blood. Bread alone is not enough by which we can live, we are nourished by every Word that comes from the mouth of God.

One does not want to divide the Eucharist and the Word of God as each, in its particular way, is the Presence of Christ, and both are central to a healthy spiritual life. Nevertheless, the spirituality of Carmel is properly said to be a spirituality of the Word. While the Eucharist is central to our lives, as it is to the life of every Christian, our spirituality cannot be said to be a Eucharistic spirituality; like all monastic spirituality it is a biblical spirituality. Indeed, in our spiritual lives the Eucharist may be the central jewel, but it is encased in the setting of the Word of God even as a precious gem is set in gold. A gem shows its brilliance best when it is in a precious setting that shows it to advantage. So too we come to appreciate the brilliant depths of the Eucharist that are shown off by the setting of the Word of God which surrounds it throughout our day. Not only the readings of the Mass, but the entire prayer of the Liturgy of the Hours and our meditation on the Word of God, enriches our appreciation for the manifestation of Christ in the Eucharistic banquet. In this sense, our spirituality, while being a spirituality of the Word, actually offers a more profound appreciation of the Eucharist than many of the pieties that are popular today. When we read our saints–Teresa of Avila, Thérèse of Lisieux, Mary Magdalene de Pazzi–we see that their appreciation for the Eucharist is drawn from their immersion in the Word of God. We cannot separate the Eucharist from the Word, but we experience the rich nourishment of the table of the Word that awakens our taste for the sweetness of the Eucharistic table.

THE PAULINE CHARACTER OF THE RULE

One of the things that has always struck me about the Rule is how rooted it is in the teaching of Saint Paul the Apostle. Albert draws on many scriptural sources, of course–the Gospels, the book of Psalms, the prophets, but there seems to be a special emphasis that he gives to the teachings of Saint Paul.

The chapters on Spiritual Warfare, chapters that I believe are very much at the heart of the Rule, are thoroughly Pauline in their thought. Craig Morrison points out in his work on the Rule that Albert was familiar with the Paul's writings and the better that we know Paul the more we recognize how his thought undergirds Albert's thought. In speaking of Spiritual Warfare, Albert draws heavily on the sixth chapter of Paul's Letter to the Ephesians. His section on work is drawn from the Second Letter to the Thessalonians. He draws on 2 Corinthians as well as the Pastoral Epistles that were attributed to Paul. But even more than the Pauline quotes on which Albert draws, Albert himself seems imbued with the spirit of Paul. Albert proposes a life of ardent faith in which we turn to Christ as our only Saviour, our sole hope of salvation. Indeed the focus of the Rule begins in Christ (a life of allegiance to Christ), goes on to climax in Christ (must always keep in mind and put into practice what our Lord said in the Gospel; your minds not on him but on Christ who has placed him over you), and concludes in Christ (Our Lord, at his second coming will reward anyone...). We, who follow the Rule, need to turn to Paul and read him constantly. The more we know Saint Paul, the better we will understand the Rule.

An outstanding example of this Pauline influence on Carmel is Elizabeth of the Trinity. Her doctrine is solid Paul all the way. It is amazing that she never formally studied the theology of Saint Paul because her mystical theology is so imbued with the Pauline vision of the Christian life that one cannot but turn to Paul's epistles when one finishes reading Elizabeth. Thérèse of the Child Jesus too is remarkably Pauline in her understanding that we are totally dependent on grace, that we come to God with empty hands. Indeed throughout almost all Carmelite spiritual literature we see a focus on Christ that bears the stamp of Paul. There is simply no where else we turn, no other hope for salvation, no other Name by which we can be saved than Jesus Christ. A Carmelite will turn to Paul as frequently as to the Gospels. Indeed, we will find that Paul opens to us the gates of a profound spiritual life that will make the Gospels come alive with ever-deeper meanings.

THE RULE AND A CHRISTOCENTRIC LIFE

In his *exordium* to the hermits, Albert calls them to lead a life that is totally directed towards Jesus Christ. They are to live a life in *obsequio Ihesu Christi*–in allegiance to Jesus Christ. A Carmelite life is a life that is focused on Jesus Christ. A Carmelite seeks only one thing, to yield himself or herself to Jesus Christ, not so they can enjoy the pleasure of knowing Christ and being loved by him, but so that they can be faithful to him and so come to eternal life.

There are those Christians who pursue Christ for the pleasure of knowing him and being loved by him and while this is often the beginning of the spiritual life, if we do not progress beyond it we are likely to fall into a heresy called quietism. Quietism is that heresy which teaches that the supreme good is being caught up in appreciating the divine love. Quietism would also teach that loving God is the highest duty to which we can give ourselves. At first glance we might be surprised that this is a heresy. It would seem to us to be a great truth. It was, in fact, embraced by many holy people and taught by many clergy, including bishops. Two of its most outstanding proponents were Archbishop Fenelon of Cambrai and Bishop Boussuet of Meaux, French bishops at the end of the seventeenth century. (Fenelon, by the way, was a very holy man, if somewhat misdirected.) When Pope Innocent XII condemned the heresy he put it quite well. Speaking of the two bishops by the names of their diocese, a common practice at the time, he declared: "Cambrai loves God too much and Meaux loves man too little." This is precisely the problem of quietism. It snaps the connection between the love of God and the love of neighbour. It creates the impression that the love of God alone suffices, when, without the love of neighbour the love of God is illusionary and not real.

For us Carmelites, Saint Teresa corrects that impression very clearly and preserves us from slipping into the false notion that the love of God can somehow be experienced as distinct from the love of neighbour. Here the famous line from the soliloquies, cited earlier, bears repeating.

"O my Jesus, how great is the love You bear the children of men, for the greatest service one can render You is to leave You for their sake and their benefit–and then You are possessed more completely. ... Whoever fails to love his neighbour, fails to love You, my Lord, since we see You showed the very great love You have for the children of Adam by shedding so much blood."[15]

Now the love of neighbour without the love of God may be a noble thing, but it is not a virtue and indeed, experience would show us that few have the strength

---

[15] Teresa of Jesus, *Soliloquies*, II 2

of altruism to go the distance with the love of neighbour unless it is rooted in the love of God. To love our neighbour for his or her own sake is a dangerous path. We will often be let down, perhaps become cynical, and eventually burn out. But a healthy spiritual life is an excellent foundation for charity because it keeps us nourished and focused so that we can see beyond the superficial face of our neighbour and learn to see him or her with the same eyes of love with which God perceives them. But to do this we must put on that same attitude which is Christ's and this requires that we ourselves undergo a profound transformation.

There are, I would suppose, a number of places to begin understanding a Christian spiritual life, but to me it is always in Galatians 2:19-20. "…I have been crucified with Christ, it is no longer I who live, but Christ lives in me. Insofar as I now live in the flesh, I live by faith in the Son of God who has loved me and given himself up for me." In this passage we see that we must die to ourselves so that Christ can be the living force in us. We must become Christ and we must let Christ become himself in us. This is a radical transformation. We must not simply become "Christlike" but must become Christ, allowing every trace of our selfish selves to be put to death so that the selflessness of Christ may take root in its place.

The unfortunate thing is that most people read this passage, and similar passages to it in Romans that speak of dying with Christ so that Christ may be raised in us, and they understand the language metaphorically. They do not understand how radical Paul's message is. We are to become Christ. We are to be transformed into Christ. What is the problem here? We believe that God, by the power of his Holy Spirit invoked in the Mass, transforms bread and wine into Christ. We become upset if anyone suggests that it is a mere metaphor. Why cannot we understand that God wishes, by the power of that same Holy Spirit, to transform us into his own Beloved Christ. Indeed, a major part of the problem is that we have separated the mystery of the Eucharist from this transformation of the Christian and left ourselves with a stunted appreciation for the Real Presence, a Christ that can be locked away in the tabernacle under the appearance of bread and ignored in his other manifestations. This is the same problem, of course with the sacrifices of the Old Testament. God wanted the hearts of his people, their lives, their very being, and they offered him bulls and goats. God wants us and we offer him bread and wine. God wants to transform us into the Flesh and Blood of his Divine Son and we back off, allowing grace to work only on the superficial levels of making us somewhat "Christ-like" rather than to make us Christ's own flesh and blood.

This may seem somewhat extreme to those whose knowledge of our Catholic Tradition is somewhat superficial, and regrettably today that even includes some of our clergy whose seminary training focused more on traditionalism than Tradition. The late distinguished Orthodox theologian, Jaroslav Pelikan, defined the difference between traditionalism and Tradition. He would say "Tradition is the living faith of the dead; traditionalism is the dead faith of the living." By this he meant, of course, that Tradition is the faith that

Some closing considerations

we still hold today, a faith that comes to us from the Apostles, the Fathers and Doctors of the Church, the Saints. On the other hand, traditionalism, is a confidence in the superficial things of our religion, a clinging to pious customs and old ways that are not rooted in the essential deposit of faith held and taught by the Church throughout the ages.

I make this distinction before I relate an experience I had some years back when a pious soul reported me to a local bishop for heresy. It was precisely on the point that I mentioned above–that God's plan is to transform us into Christ. The Christian is called to become Christ, not metaphorically, no more metaphorically than the Eucharistic Bread and Wine become Christ, but in a very Real way. The particular statement to which the pious lady objected, and was sure was heresy, was "God became human so that humans might become God." That is a profound statement. God, in the second Person of the Blessed Trinity became human so that we might become Divine. Christ becomes us so that we might become Christ. In the end the charge of heresy did not hold up, of course. The quote after all is not mine, it is from Saint Athanasius. It is the Tradition of the Church.

Our Carmelite vocation is Christocentric precisely to this point. We are called to be transformed into Christ. We can not do this ourselves. Only the Holy Spirit can do this. And, unfortunately, it seems for most of us to take a lifetime, and even beyond this life, to come to its perfection. But that is not the problem. God has all eternity to achieve his plan for us if need be. Our life in Carmel is about this transformation. We keep our eyes focused on Christ. In reading his word, in meditating on his word, in praying his word, we gradually learn how, like Christ, to surrender ourselves completely to the will of God for us. This requires a total focus on Christ. He is our only focus. All else points to him and he points to the Father. Our love and devotion to his Mother ultimately directs us not to her, but to him. Our admiration for the saints of our Carmelite family directs us not to them but him. Our desire for union with him is not oriented towards our spiritual pleasure, but towards the transformation of ourselves in him that union brings about as Saint John of the Cross expresses so well in the poem, the *Ascent of Mount Carmel*. Indeed, in this journey into Christ we will experience not only moments of joy, but more importantly moments of trial, of seeming abandonment, of great darkness as our selfish desire for even spiritual pleasure is purged so that we can give without hope of return, for Christ will not live in us until we are able to love without demanding that we be loved.

The best part of this transformation into Christ is that it is all but invisible to those around us unless they look in the one right place. We do not seem more holy, more spiritual. Our talk is not filled with pious thoughts, our time given incessantly to prayer. We don't lose our sense of humour, in fact, if we haven't a sense of humour we might gain one. The only sign is that we are more and more conformed to the Will of our Father in heaven and the one manifestation of this is an ever-increasing charity for others. Slowly we become more patient, more compassionate, more willing

Some closing considerations

to go out of our way for others. We have a certain understanding of the faults and weaknesses, even the sins, of others. We are not inclined to judgment, much less to gossip. People who once annoyed us we now can tolerate without any visible sign of irritation. Most people around us will probably not notice the change, but we can see it. The unwise expect spiritual growth to be in an increase in piety and they are impressed by devotion, but the unwise also expect material wealth to be expressed in good taste and we all know that is not the case. Charity and charity alone is the measuring stick of holiness. To be Christlike is to become ourselves an incarnation of the Divine Love.

A FINAL REFLECTION

SPIRITUAL WARFARE: THE CARMELITE VOCATION TO WIN THE WORLD FOR CHRIST

It was the Friday evening before Palm Sunday and we Friars at Sant'Alberto, the International Carmelite Centre in Rome, were gathered for Lectio Divina.[16] We were preparing to celebrate the entry of Christ into Jerusalem by meditating together on the age-old story of Christ's entrance into Jerusalem as it is related in the Gospel of Saint Luke. We sat there in the common room, our circle of chairs putting us face to face with one another, Italians, Americans, Maltese, Indians, Africans, Indonesians, Spaniards, Poles, Czechs, Brazilians, Irish, English–Carmelites all, and from all parts of the globe. We sat there silently attentive to the Word of God, as we are called to by the Rule of Saint Albert, that precious letter from a long-ago bishop that has guided us Carmelites on the path of following Jesus for almost eight centuries. We sat there together drawing from the peace which God places in the hearts of each person who attentively listens to his Word. As the Gospel was slowly read, we listened, attentively and with closed eyes, to the story which has for centuries stirred

---

[16] This chapter was originally printed in *Carmel in the World*. It is reprinted here with some minor changes.

the hearts of believers. We heard of the disciples sent to retrieve this tethered donkey from an unknown man. We heard of the palms waved and cloaks scattered on the ground. We heard that if the crowd were silent, the stones themselves would call out. But most of all we heard how the Lord would come into his city mounted on a donkey, the foal of an ass.

I had heard this Gospel before so many times, and never before was the significance of that donkey so clear as it was that afternoon in our *Lectio*. I had never really thought about the donkey. It seemed simply a matter regarding the normal beast that one would ride, sort of like borrowing a friend's Toyota today. But this day the deeper theological significance struck me. I listened as the words of Zechariah 9:9-10 were read.

> "See your king shall come to you.
> A just saviour is he,
> Meek, and riding on an ass.
> On a colt, the foal of an ass.
> He shall banish the chariot from Ephraim,
> And the horse from Jerusalem.
> The warrior's bow shall be banished,
> And he shall proclaim peace to the nations."

Yes, the Lord would come into his city as the prophets foretold, mounted not on the horse of the warrior, not riding in the war chariot of the king, but riding the donkey–the animal of peace. When Jesus chose to make his entry to Jerusalem he signalled that he would be a very different kind of King, a servant King, the Bringer of Peace.

Jerusalem, the city of peace, has always longed for, but rarely found, peace. The name of the city is ironic, a name drawn from the same ancient roots as the Hebrew word *Shalom* and the Arabic word, Salaam, both words meaning peace. Yet this city named for peace been fought over for three thousand years–since the time that David conquered the city from the Jebusites. Down through the centuries people have fought mercilessly for this city, Babylonians, Greeks, and Romans, the Persians in 614, the Arabs in 638, the Crusaders in 1099, the armies of the great Muslim general Saladin in 1187. The war continues in our own time. The city named for peace has known far too much violence. But what is disturbing and should give us pause, if one knows one's history, is the role that Christians have played in bringing violence to Jerusalem. Violence and warfare did not begin with Christianity, of course, and earlier conquests, most notably the Roman overthrow of the Temple in 70 AD, the suppression of the Shimon Bar Kochba Revolt (132-135), and the Persian conquest of 614 were incredibly bloody. But when one turns to the Crusades, one can see Christians behaving with the violence of those who have never heard the message of Christ. The heritage of this Crusader violence is with us still today in the terrorist attacks on the once-Christian nations of the West, and the West's violent confrontation with Islam in Iraq and Afghanistan. We need to look at our history and learn from it. While we in the west have been taught to look to Islam as the source of violence between the Christian west and Muslim countries of the Near East, the truth of history is very different.

During my doctoral studies at New York University, I was fortunate to take a course on the history of Islam. The professor was an Arab, but a Catholic, and from an Egyptian family that had been Christian for centuries. In her course she introduced us to the most current literature available on Islamic history, predominately the work of European and American scholars who were not themselves Muslims. Of course we also read the English translation of the Qur'an and other Muslim texts. It was an eye-opener to take a serious look at Islam from a scholarly point of view. It shattered many stereotypes and has prepared me to better understand the bridges of dialogue that Pope John Paul II tried to build with the Muslim world.

Mohammed himself was remarkably well-disposed towards Christianity. He most likely had learned to read and write from a Christian monk, and the influence of that monk is strong on Islam and its holy book, the Qur'an. Mohammed's tutor was not an orthodox Christian, but a Nestorian, and it is a very Nestorian Jesus who shows up in the Qur'an. Nestorians are named after a fifth-century bishop, Nestorius, who had an exaggerated idea of the divinity of Jesus. He was troubled over the problem of how can an immortal God die, and thus he had to find a way to separate out the humanity of Jesus from his divinity. Nestorius taught that Jesus was two persons, one divine and one human, and the connection between the divine and the human was superficial, a matter of external appearance. Building on this, the followers of Nestorius believed that only the human Jesus suffered and died on the Cross, but that the Eternal Word, the second Person of the Blessed Trinity, escaped death. It is a surprise to many Christians to discover that while Muslims do not accept the divinity of Christ, the Qur'an, following the Gospels of Matthew and Luke, teaches the Virgin Birth of Jesus. The Qur'an also teaches that God, at the last minute, delivered Jesus from the cross, substituting a look-alike in his place, reflecting the Nestorian unease about his death. While Mohammed drew on Nestorian ideas for the Qur'an, he did not distinguish between orthodox and Nestorian Christians in his writings, and both Jesus and the Virgin Mary play no insignificant role in the revelation which Mohammed claimed to have received from the Angel Gabriel and recorded in his sacred book. In fact, some years ago while celebrating the annual feast of the Madonna with the Carmelites at Trapani in Sicily, I was surprised to see large numbers of Muslims from North Africa reverently standing along the procession route as we carried Our Lady's image through the streets. It was the first time that I was aware of how important the Blessed Virgin is to Muslims and the honour they show her as the Virgin Mother of Jesus whom they regard as a great prophet, second only to their own.

Mohammed did not see Christians or Jews as "infidels," but as "people of the book," that is, as people who had received the revelation from God that prepared the way for the revelation he brought. While Mohammed declared that non-believers should be given the choice of accepting Islam or facing death, he taught his followers that Christians and Jews, as "people of the book" were not to be coerced into accepting Islam.

God had spoken through Moses and through Jesus, and if–in his opinion–their disciples had distorted the revelation, it did not negate the Word God has spoken through the Mosaic Law and the Christian Gospel. This is not to say that being a Christian did not convey legal disabilities in Muslim lands. Mohammed said that it was just to make Christians and Jews carry the brunt of the taxation, that Muslim governors should tax them more heavily than they did the Islamic faithful, but should not force them to accept Islam by threat of violence. Perhaps surprisingly to modern people, millions of Christians and Jews carried this tax burden for centuries without abandoning their religion to escape it. Indeed, the Christian populations of the Near East and North Africa, and even Spain, for the most part accepted the Islamic conquest with a minimum of resistance and often became key officials in the Islamic Caliphate but retained their Christian religion and were able to practice it openly. Saint John Damascene, for example, was the chief financial officer of the Damascus Caliphate before becoming a monk. It was the Greeks and the Syrians–both Christian peoples–who had the knowledge of medicine, science, mathematics, and philosophy, and while the Arabs were quick learners, they patiently and respectfully learned from their Christian mentors. Intellectual life flourished in Muslim Spain and Muslim Syria and even in the Baghdad Caliphate because of the interplay between Jewish, Muslim, and Christian cultures and religions fostered by the tolerance of Muslim rulers.

Shortly after the death of Mohammed, Arab conquerors overran much of the Byzantine half of the old

Roman Empire, including the lands in which Christ had once lived. The Muslim invasions did not destroy the Christian Holy places nor threaten Christian life there. The Muslims were in fact benevolent invaders whom the population came to prefer over the Byzantine Greeks. When the Muslims took the Jerusalem from the Byzantines in 638, it was without bloodshed. Upon entering the city, the Caliph 'Umar went directly to the Church of the Holy Sepulchre, the basilica that had been built by Constantine three centuries earlier, to pay his respects to Christ who, as I have said, is regarded in Islam as a great prophet. 'Umar was invited by the Christian Patriarch, Sophronius, to say his prayers inside the church, but refused lest his followers decide that the Christian shrine must then become a mosque. Instead he spread his prayer carpet in the courtyard in front of the basilica and knelt there for his prayers so that the Christians would not lose their holy site. For many centuries the Muslims and the Christians peacefully coexisted in the Holy Land. Christians often served the caliphs as their physicians, their treasurers, their tutors, and as ambassadors to Christian kings and rulers. While Syria-Palestine was subject to the Muslim caliph at Damascus, the people, for the most part, remained Christian. (Until the establishment of the State of Israel and the consequent disenfranchisement of the Palestinian people, about half the Arabs in the Holy Land were Christian. Some towns, such as Bethlehem and Nazareth were almost entirely Christian. In the last half-century, most Christian Arabs have fled to Europe and the Americas to be free of the legal disabilities and second-class citizenship that have been imposed on Arabs in the State of Israel.) Most of the Christian Arabs in the Holy Land, both at the time of the Muslim invasion and in the fifty-five years of Israeli rule are Eastern Christians, Syrian or Greek Orthodox, though there are significant groups of Eastern Rite Catholics, and a small community of Latin, or today we say Roman, Rite Catholics. The Latin Patriarch, Michel Sabbah, much to the annoyance of the Israeli officials, is himself a Palestinian Arab.

Within a century of Mohammed's death, a huge Islamic empire had been carved out of the Byzantine and old Roman worlds. From Syria in the North down through Palestine, Lebanon, Iraq and Iran, the Saudi Peninsula over to Egypt and across North Africa, up through Spain and Portugal, Muslim armies had conquered a huge portion of the world, its wealth, and its peoples. When they were finally turned back from overrunning Europe at a key battle at Tours in central France in the middle of the eighth century, Islam had reached its high-water mark for the Middle Ages. While many of the conquered people accepted Islam at once, the vast majority of Christians held on to their faith. In the Iberian peninsula, including modern Spain and Portugal, Christians and Jews held on to their faiths almost universally, but worked well together with the Muslims in creating a very sophisticated and cultured society where the three religions openly dialogued and exchanged theological and philosophical insights. In Egypt the Coptic Church, the religion of the indigenous people of Egypt implanted by the missionary activities of Saint Mark in Alexandria, continued–and continues today. While the majority of people in Egypt today are Arabs–and Muslims–the native Egyptian people, the descendents of the ancient Egyptians, mostly belong to the Coptic Orthodox Church under the Pope of Alexandria. Orthodox monks have survived at the ancient monastery of Saint Catherine in the Sinai, site of the burning bush, as well as other monasteries throughout the Islamic Near East. Though much reduced in size through recent emigrations, Syrian and Palestinian Christian communities have remained in their ancient homelands, as have the Maronites of Lebanon. While many Palestinian and Lebanese Christians have fled their homelands to America, Britain, Australia, and Western Europe, their Muslim fellow-nationalists have for the most part remained, changing the religious balance of these ancient lands. Christian Arabs have also adapted to western culture more enthusiastically than Muslim Arabs and quickly become integrated into the societies to which they have emigrated whereas the Muslim immigrants tend to remain separate from the cultures of their new societies. Christian immigrants loose the "Arab" identity and become French or American or British, while Muslim immigrants retain their distinct identities and often find themselves in tension with their non-Muslim neighbours. But in the Near East centuries of Islamic Rule had not destroyed, nor for the most part tried to destroy, these Christian Churches that go back to Apostolic times. Similarly, indigenous Christian Churches survived in Iraq and Iran. The Syrian Patriarchate at Damascus flourishes and the Syrian Orthodox Church is one of the Eastern

Churches has been most cordial in its ecumenical dialogue with the Roman Catholic Church. It was only in Saudi Arabia, the sacred homeland of Islam where the revelation was given to Mohammed, that Jews and Christians were, and still are, barred from practicing their faith. But we are getting ahead of our story.

The eleventh century was a time of drastic and often calamitous change. On a positive note, the tenth century had seen western Europeans, principally from Italian coastal cities, establishing trading posts in the Holy Land to bring back the elegant fabrics and spices that the West began to covet. More and more Europeans began pouring into the coastal cities, and into Jerusalem as well, seeking commercial ties, but also coming as pilgrims. Western Christians even opened up "hospitals" or pilgrim shelters for pilgrims coming from what is today Italy and France and England.

One of these hospitals, the Hospital of Saint John of Jerusalem, had been founded at the behest of Pope Saint Gregory in the year 600–thirty years before the Arab conquest. The Muslims allowed the hospice to continue, and in fact, to expand. The Emperor Charlemagne enlarged the hospital and added a library to it around the year 800. In 1005, the Mad Caliph, al-Hakim destroyed it and about three thousand other Christian sites in the Holy Land. However in 1023, the new Caliph Ali az-Zahir gave the Christians permission to rebuild the Hospital and it was given to the charge of Benedictine monks. In 1080 a new brotherhood was established there that would later become a new Religious Order composed of knights who protected and helped the pilgrims. They continue today as the Order of Malta, or as they are sometimes called, the Knights of Malta.

Al-Hakim's attack on the Hospital of Saint John of Jerusalem was not his only act of violence against Christianity. He also ordered the tomb of Christ to be demolished. It was razed to the ground, sparking a fury among Christians everywhere. In 1054 there was a horrific split between the Greek and Roman Churches with mutual excommunications being hurled about like thunderbolts. In 1072, the Caliph closed Jerusalem to Christian pilgrims. Finally, in 1095 Pope Urban II called on the Kings and Princes of Europe to mount a military campaign to restore the Holy Land to Christian authority. Urban hoped to stop the constant warfare among the Catholic princes in Europe by focusing their military strength outward toward an external enemy. The Arabs made an excellent target for this external aggression. The Caliphate was not stable. They were in a period of political chaos and military decline. Their defeat would restore the holy shrines to Christian, and Catholic, control. Pope Urban also hoped that by defeating the Arabs on the southern border of the Byzantine Empire, he might effect a reconciliation between the Greek Orthodox peoples of the East and the Western Catholics, healing the schism which had begun over forty years earlier. Unfortunately, this part of his plan was never realized, and in fact the barbarity of the Crusaders towards the non-Catholic Christians, especially during the 1204 Sack of Constantinople in the Fourth Crusade, seems to have permanently damaged the relations between the estranged sister Churches of

Orthodoxy and Rome. But to explore that tragedy would take us too far afield of our story.

Pope Urban's Crusade was an exercise in violence before it even left Europe. Unwilling to wait to get to Syria-Palestine before the slaughter began, Crusaders traveling down the German Rhine valley towards Italy and the ships that would carry them across the sea to the Holy Land, attacked Jewish communities and slaughtered any non-Christians they could find to whet their appetite for "infidel" blood. Arriving in the Holy Land, the conquest of the Land for Christ was swift–and brutal. On July 15, 1099 the Crusader armies seized Jerusalem and the Latin Kingdom was established. Muslims were slaughtered in the tens of thousands, the streets ran with blood. The chronicles say that the blood was up to the bellies of the horses on the Temple Mount as the residents of Jerusalem, women and children as well as the men, were indiscriminately slain. The small Jewish population in the Holy Land also suffered from the Crusading armies. Even Christians whose rites and traditions were different than those familiar to the Crusaders were victims of the violence, often being put the sword while seeking refuge at the altars of their churches. It was markedly different from 'Umar's conquest of Jerusalem four-and-a-half centuries earlier. The Crusaders thought they were restoring Jerusalem to its rightful King, but the Prince of Peace must have looked on with horror at what was being done in his name. It was a tragic witness to how far those who bore the cross on their shields and armour had departed from the teachings of Christ and the faith of the apostolic Church.

A Final Reflection

The victory was bloody but the conquest was not as long lasting as the Crusaders had hoped. Eighty-eight years later the Crusaders lost the city to the brilliant Seljuk Turk General Saladin. Thousands and thousands of Christians, ordinary people–men and women and children, merchants and traders and pilgrims and hermits and priests–were stranded behind enemy lines. But this time, at the hands of the Muslim Saladin, there was no blood bath. A modest ransom was set, upon payment the captive could leave Muslim territory and go to Tyre to await the boats that were evacuating the Europeans from the Holy Land. In Jerusalem, there were twenty thousand Christians too poor to pay the ransom. Saladin relented and ordered that they simply be released.

Saladin did not stop his conquests at Jerusalem. He was determined to drive the Latin Christians from Syria Palestine, though his Syrian and Greek Orthodox subjects were welcomed to stay, and he gave to them the control of the ancient churches which the Crusaders had taken from them for the Catholics. In the process he won the loyalty of those non-Latin Christians. There was no stopping Saladin's army and finally the Crusaders had been driven to the port of Tyre, with their backs to the sea. All the western Europeans fled for protection, waiting for the boats that would take them back to Europe. Monks and bishops, knights and squires, prostitutes and washerwomen, merchants and farmers, were all cooped up together waiting for the ships to come and bring them back from this failed experiment of the Crusades.

But the Crusaders were ready for yet another try. When the ships did come, they brought the Kings of

France and England, and the Emperor as well. The War was on again! The Third Crusade! It was fairly successful for the Crusaders, for while they never recaptured Jerusalem, they were able to carve out for themselves a large area in what is now northern Israel, Lebanon and western Syria. For yet another century they would rule this kingdom. On its southern border, not far from Muslim lines, stands Mount Carmel. And it is here where our hermits come to be.

These hermits had not themselves been Crusaders, or even the foot soldiers who accompanied the knights off to the Crusades. The Crusaders came from knightly and noble families and were they to have had a conversion and opted for a Religious Life, it would not have been the life of lay hermits. Lay hermits were drawn from the non-noble commercial classes–merchants and traders and artisans and craftsmen. Pilgrims might settle at the end of their journey and become hermits. Some hermits came over from Europe on pilgrimage and decided to remain as hermits in the land of Christ. Nobility wishing a more religious life entered either the monastic orders such as the Cistercians and Benedictines, or in the Holy Land particularly, knights would be expected to join the Military Orders such as the Knights Templar or the Knights of the Hospital of Saint John of Jerusalem. These were Religious Orders specifically for knights. They remained knights while becoming full-fledged Religious. They had solemn vows, wore a habit, and sat in choir while their chaplains solemnly recited the Offices according to monastic customs. The members of these Military Orders lived a monastic life in their conventual buildings, eating in a common refectory, and following a Rule written specifically for them. The Cistercian abbot, Saint Bernard of Clairvaux, adapted the Rule of Saint Benedict for the Knights Templar. Blessed Raymond du Puy wrote the Rule for the Knights of the Hospital of Saint John of Jerusalem, basing it on the Rule of Saint Augustine. But while they had become Religious, they were also knights, and they got on their horses and went into battle to defend the land for Christ. The foot-soldiers who accompanied the knights were welcomed as Lay Brothers in the Military Orders. Frankly, in the state of war in which the Crusader army found itself, it could not have its numbers being depleted by knights, of whom there were less than two thousand in the Holy Land, going off and laying down their arms as monks or hermits.

There had been many western Christian hermits in the Holy Land before Saladin's conquest and most of them fled to the safety of Tyre when the Muslim general defeated the Christians at the Battle of Hattin in 1187. After Richard the Lionhearted and Philip Augustus won back the land in the third Crusade, the hermits were free to go and re-establish themselves once again in the rocky fastness of their hermitages. Some went back to the desert of the Temptation, even though it was behind Muslim lines. And some went to the Jordan River Valley, again under Muslim domination. But others chose to stay under the protection of the Crusaders and so it came to be that several–we don't know exactly how many–found their way to a lovely little valley, called the wadi 'ain es-Siah on the south west face of the mountain range known as Carmel, just a few miles above the sea.

It was a tranquil place, close enough to the sea to enjoy the breezes. It was watered by two natural wells or fountains, one traditionally ascribed to the prophet Elijah who had lived on this mountain almost two thousand years before. There was good land for gardens. And as they were not far off the pilgrim road that led down to Jerusalem from the Crusader capital city, Acre, they could expect a steady stream of visitors to their little settlement and its simple church.

We really don't know exactly when hermits began to settle in the wadi 'ain es-Siah. It was most probably only after the peace treaty of 1191 that a permanent foundation could have been made. Had there been any hermits living there before, and there are no evidence of any, they would have had to leave and flee to Tyre before the armies of Saladin after the debacle of Hattin in 1187. On the other hand, hermits had to have settled there and organized themselves into some sort of a loose community before 1214, because that was the year that the Patriarch Albert of Jerusalem died, and it was Albert who gave them this *Pattern for Life* that today we call The Rule. The only dating we can give with any assurance is that the *Pattern for Life* was written sometime during Albert's stay in the Holy Land, between his arrival in 1206 until his death in 1214.

As was stated earlier, we do not know when these hermits came nor do we know who they were. No names survive, except the first initial, "B.", of the leader of the community at the time the Patriarch Albert gave them their *Pattern for Life*. Some of our hermits were undoubtedly pilgrims who had come to the Holy Land and decided to stay there. Some–perhaps–had been hermits in Europe and came on pilgrimage to the Holy Land. Others might have come to the Holy Land for other purposes–perhaps looking for fame or fortune in the Crusader world–and having found it, realized how vain are the prizes of this world, that only Christ can satisfy the Christian heart. And some probably came excited by the glory of these wars for Christ, and once they saw the violence and injustice of war, realized that the world can be won for Christ not by bloodshed, but only by living out his Gospel in all its demands. The Gospel of Christ is something worth dying for, but it is a betrayal of all that Christ taught to think that we could kill for it. After all, the Christian realizes that the only war in which one can find justice is the war within one's own heart, the war which God and his angels must fight for us to deliver us from the only true enemy. Saint Paul speaks of this war in the sixth chapter of his letter to the Ephesians, and as we have seen, this text was and remains central to Carmelite Spirituality.

The hermits on Mount Carmel were part of the vast movement of men and women who had come to win the holy land for Christ, to make Christ king of the land in which he had been born, had lived, and had died. Some in this movement were knights and soldiers. They took up military arms against the Muslim foe. But our hermits did not play an active role in the Crusades, they did not espouse the military solution to this challenge. They turned to the letter of Saint Paul to the Ephesians and found there an alternative form of warfare. They were so convinced of the need for spiritual warfare that they incorporated this call of the Apostle into their Rule, albeit in paraphrased language. Both the scripture and the long tradition in the writings of the Church Fathers declared that the real battle was not a battle between nations, or religions, or cultures, but a battle between heaven and hell for the souls of men and women. "For our struggle is not with flesh and blood, but with the principalities, with the powers, with the world rulers of this present darkness, with the evil spirits in the heavens" (Ephesians 6:12). The hermits were sceptical that the knights would be able to win the land for Christ and history would show that even this noble cause was doomed to failure, as the weapons of knighthood were the wrong weapons for the work of God. The knights had tried to take the land, and almost lost their holdings completely with the victory of Saladin. Even now their hold on the land was tenuous. Christ's kingdom is not a kingdom of this world and it made no sense to the hermits that knights, even pious ones such as the Knights Templar or the Knights Hospitaler, were going to be able to win this eternal kingdom through very temporal means. The hermits consecrated themselves to a countercultural form of warfare in which they were confident the victory for Christ could truly be won. Even as Paul had told them that the real enemy was not flesh and blood but the Evil One and his minions–the earthly powers and principalities–so too Paul had instructed them as to how to wage this warfare.

The idea that the monk was to clothe himself in the armour of God so as to wage warfare against the enemy in the great spiritual battle was not a new insight for the Carmelite. John Cassian had used this image in his conferences he had given to his monks centuries earlier and these conferences, being read with regularity in every monastic refectory in the Latin West, long had formed the backbone of western spirituality. The Lay hermits of the twelfth and thirteenth centuries were guided by the thought of Cassian who was in many ways a figure that spoke to their spirit more than Benedict, Anselm, Bernard or the later monastic authors. Our hermits in the wadi 'ain es-Siah understood what their lay contemporaries did not, namely that the battle, the true battle was not with Muslims in the Holy Land any more than it is with terrorists today. The true battle is the battle of good and evil, the battle between God and that which is not God, and the ground of this battle is not the ground under Jerusalem or the air over New York. This battle is described by Paul and is as true for our days as it was for Paul, and as it was for those hermits in Crusader Palestine.

> "Therefore put on the armour of God
> that you may be able to resist on the evil day
> and, having done everything, hold your ground.
> So stand fast with your loins girded in truth,
> clothed with integrity as a breastplate,
> and your feet shod in readiness for the Gospel of peace
> in all circumstances hold faith as a shield,
> to quench all the flaming arrows of the Evil One,
> and take the helmet of salvation
> and the Sword of the Spirit, which is the Word of God." (Ephesians 6: 10-17).

The hermits saw that their vocation, not as Carmelites but as Christians, called them to clothe themselves in God's own armour, that is, to take up the weapons of God himself against evil. Like Paul when he composed the passage, the hermits would have been familiar with the Old Testament roots of this idea of the Divine Warrior and his armour. Paul did not weave his admonition to spiritual warfare in Ephesians out of his imagination–it came from his deep faith in the Word that God has spoken in generations past, the faith he had received from his Jewish roots. This armour of God is a theme that one finds in the Hebrew scriptures, most notably in Isaiah 59:17, when God sees the tide turning in favour of sin and, finding no champion to take up the cause of right, God himself becomes the warrior

> "He saw that there was no one,
> And was appalled that there was none to intervene.
> So his own arm brought about the victory,
> And his justice lent him its support.
> He put on justice as his breastplate,
> Salvation, as the helmet on his head.
> He clothed himself with garments of vengeance,
> Wrapped himself in a mantle of zeal." (Isaiah 59:16-17)

Yes, God himself became the warrior against the evil that was swallowing the land in sin. And what was the sin that God was fighting? Look in Isaiah 59 and you will see.

> "Your hands are stained with blood, your fingers with guilt. Your lips speak falsehood, and your tongue ut-

ters deceit. No one brings suit justly, no one pleads truthfully ... the way of peace they know not...their ways they have made crooked. Threatening outrage and apostasy, uttering words of falsehood...truth stumbles in the public square ... honesty is lacking...." (Isaiah 59: 3-15)

It is sobering to read this. Modern Christians think that the sins that shall bring down the world around us are private sins, especially sins of a sexual nature. While these sins are indeed wicked, and undermine the stability of society, we see that it was social sin that was bringing the world of Isaiah's day to ruin, and it was this social sin that God was determined to root out. We can recognize some of the same social sins today–violence, false testimony, failure of public figures to be truthful, unjust legal actions. Perhaps this is a bit of a digression from our main theme, but the blindness to social sin–indeed the acceptance of social sin in our society–is a far greater danger to peace and stability in our world than most people today acknowledge. We have been deceived into turning a blind eye to the public and corporate sins of our society while focusing only on the weaknesses of individuals. We must ask ourselves if this blindness has not led to the very heart being eaten out of our societies, leaving our world in ruins. How much has our acceptance of violence, for example, in entertainment, in video games, even in the news, immunized us against the tremendous human suffering of so many people in our planet? How immune have we become to public figures lying to us while behind our backs their friends have looted corporate treasuries leaving workers without pension funds and depriving investors of their returns? How much do we ignore wars that cost the lives of the poor, soldier and civilian alike, and make rich the politicians whose companies have government contracts to "rebuild" the war-devastated nations? How much have the nuisance suits clogged our courts from administering genuine justice, and how much have fraudulent suits and outrageous claims driven medical costs beyond the reach of average people? If this seems to you to be extraneous to spirituality, remember that in the battle with the cosmic powers, the Evil One is as likely to wear a business suit as a caftan, as likely to be found in politics as in Islamic fundamentalism, and may well attend church every Sunday.

We have yet another, indeed earlier, reference to the Divine Armour in Isaiah 11:4-9, when it is mentioned in the context of the Messiah's battle to establish peace. The Kingdom of Judah was, at the time, threatened by Assyria. The Northern kingdom, Israel, had already been punished for its sins, had been defeated by Assyria, and its citizens had been led away in slavery to disappear forever from history, the so-called ten lost tribes of Israel. What were the sins that brought down the nation of those ten tribes who had once been God's chosen ones? According to the prophet Amos they were again sins of social injustice.

"Hear this, you who trample upon the needy
and destroy the poor of the land!" (Amos 8:4)

"You who oppose the weak
And abuse the needy." (Amos 4:1)

Israel was brought down because of the way it oppressed its poor, and Isaiah, in chapter ten, sees the suffe-

A Final Reflection

ring of the poor as threatening the security of Judah in the same way. But God promises a redeemer who will address the suffering of the poor and at the same time deliver his people from their enemy. And he shall do it wearing the armour of God–girt round his waist with justice and belted with faithfulness.

> "He shall judge the poor with justice,
> And decide aright for the land's afflicted.
> He shall strike the ruthless with the rod of his mouth,
> And with the breath of his lips he shall slay the wicked.
> Justice shall be the band around his waist, and faithfulness a belt upon his hips.
> Then the wolf shall be the guest of the lamb,
> And the leopard shall lie down with the kid.
> The calf and the bear shall be neighbours,
> Together their young shall rest.
> The lion shall eat hay like the ox.
> The baby shall lay by the cobra's den,
> And the child lay his hand on the adder's lair.
> There shall be no harm or ruin on all my holy mountain,
> For the earth shall be filled with the knowledge of the Lord
> As water covers the sea." (Isaiah 11: 4-9)

We see that the Messiah will destroy the evildoers, but he will do it by his Word, not by earthly weapons, and the fruit of his victory will be a reign of peace. The armour he wears in this battle is justice and faithfulness.

There is yet one more passage that deals with the same theme of the Lord putting on his armour to avenge his people. The Book of Wisdom declares that the Lord will wage war on behalf of the just, protecting them from their enemies and lists the weapons that the Lord will use in this struggle.

> "He shall shelter them (the just) with his right hand,
> And protect them with his arm.
> He shall take his zeal for armour
> And he shall arm creation to requite the enemy.
> He shall don justice for a breastplate
> And shall wear sure judgment for a helmet
> He shall make invincible rectitude as a shield
> And whet his sudden anger for a sword."
> (Wisdom 5:16-19)

Paul looks around at the world of his day and he saw this battle between good and evil continuing. He remembered that the armour of God is still there for his readers to take up in their day, even as they were there for Isaiah and for the author of the Book of Wisdom. What are these weapons? Paul went through the passages from the Hebrew Scriptures and picked out several of God's weapons. Justice is still the breastplate and salvation is the helmet. ("Justice" and "integrity" are equivalent theological terms in the Hebrew scriptures. Justice, righteousness, and holiness are all related theological concepts. In sacred scripture, the just person, the righteous person, and the holy one are all one and the same.) Other weapons change. Faith–a major theme in Paul–replaces invincible rectitude as

A Final Reflection

the shield, and the Word of God replaces anger as the sword, in this case the Word of God being given that wonderful appellation, the "Sword of the Spirit." The loins are to be girded with truth, replacing justice and faithfulness around the hips. And Paul adds something new to the armour–as surely as the Gospel itself was added new to the Law and the Prophets–shoes in which to bring the Gospel of peace. And so we have the weapons with which we are to fight the battle, the weapons that God himself uses: truth, integrity, the Gospel of peace, faith, salvation, and the Sword of the Spirit–the Word of God. These are dramatic words. They were challenging words for the Ephesians who lived amid the violence of the Roman world. They were challenging words for the hermits among the violence of the Crusades. They are challenging words for us, amidst the violence of international terrorism.

We must ask ourselves: what does it mean to protect ourselves with truth? Pilate may have asked cynically when he questioned Christ: "what is truth?" But Pilate's cynicism aside, the question is fair. What is truth? To whom can we turn for truth? The Apostles knew where we could turn for Truth: "You, Lord, have the words of everlasting life. We have come to believe and are convinced that you are the Holy One of God" (John 6:68-69). One lesson I have learned as a historian is whether it be Nero explaining the fire of Rome, Henry VIII breaking his nation from Papal authority, or England's treatment of her American colonies, governments have shown themselves unreliable in telling truth to their citizens. At best, what today we call a "spin" is put on the "facts" that politicians offer their constituents. And can we expect better? Truth in our temporal order changes from day to day, or rather what we know about the truth changes from day to day. Weapons of mass destruction may or may not have existed. Our leaders may or may not have known whether or not they existed. The information given to them may or may not have been based on solid evidence. Such is not the level at which truth can be found, at least the Truth that we are seeking. The shifting sand of world politics is not the Truth of which Saint Paul speaks. There is a Truth beyond our small and all-too-often partial truths. There is Truth that is constant in a world of Viet Nams and Iraqs, in a world of Rwandan and Nazi genocides, in a world of terrorism and imperialism. The Gospel stands eternally True, true in all ages, true in every situation. Christ's truth is the Truth in which we must gird ourselves, protecting ourselves from being fatally wounded by the weapons of the Father of Lies. In other words, whatever the politics of the moment, the Christian keeps his eyes focused on the Gospel and the unchanging message of Christ. In his battle to win the world for Christ, the Christian does not compromise the message of the Gospel, for to win any battle or any war at the price of abandoning the words of Christ would be to loose all. The Christian never looses sight that there is one God who is Father of All, and that friend and foe alike are brothers and sisters, children of the same heavenly Father. This makes the Christian cast a very different eye on warfare. Whatever divides us from one another–nationality, religion, and even the deepest enmity of the most violent war–is not as strong as what unites us, the One God who loves us all as his children and wants with all his Divine Being for us to find together a way to peace. The Christian knows from his or her faith that the Truth is the solidarity of the human family, regardless of political, racial, and religious differences.

Paul says that we need to put on Integrity as our breastplate. Some translations use justice for integrity, others holiness. In the Greek of the New Testament, they are all rooted in the same virtue. Justice means being right with God. We are set right with God, Paul tells us in his letters to the Romans and to the Galatians, not by our own efforts or virtues, but by faith in Christ. In other words, we are set right with God when we take Jesus at his word, not simply professing faith with our tongue, but committing ourselves in faith to live according to the principles which Christ teaches us, not according to self-interest, or common sense, or the demands of society and law. In all that we do, we need to be able to stand before the throne of God not as victors in any earthly sense, but clothed in the righteousness of the children of God. Again, if we compromise our fidelity to the Gospel in order to win this war against the Evil One, the Evil One in fact will have scored a victory, and we will have lost all. So in this battle we need to turn the other cheek. We need to pray for our persecutors and to love our enemies. We need not to meet violence with violence, but to be people of an immense forgiveness and a profound patience, for to do anything less would be to fail Christ by abandoning his Word for some lesser strategy. We must be merciful even as our heavenly Father is merciful. We must forgive even as we have been forgiven. Only faith gives us the courage to resist returning evil for evil, eye for eye, tooth for tooth.

Our feet, Paul tells us, are to be shod with the shoes of the Gospel of peace. We need to bring the message of the Good News, the message that in Jesus Christ there is a lasting and profound peace, to all people. "How beautiful on the mountain," the prophet tells us, "are the feet of those who bring the good news" (Isaiah 52:7). The Good News, the Gospel, is the message of a victory, the victory of Christ over sin and death, not only in the eternal sense, but here in this temporal order. God's plan for our salvation is not only about eternity, it is a plan for salvation in the temporal order. Christ came to break the power over us that leads us to destroy one another. We must witness to this Gospel of Victory by being men and women who are consecrated to peace. To bring any other message but the victory of Christ and his kingdom of peace is to betray Christ. There is no Good News that is authentically Christian other than the message of peace. Peace will conquer violence but only when the disciples of Christ abandon violence and arm themselves only with the peace that Christ offers each person who believes in him. He does not give us peace as the world offers peace–a brief tranquillity–but he offers us the peace that can be had only when God is given his reign over us. He offers us a new way to live together with one another in this world.

Now, peace is not merely a cessation of warfare, but rather the establishment of a situation in which all is as God has created it to be. In other words, just because there is no warfare at a given moment or in a given place, does not mean there is peace. Peace is not the absence of something, but rather the presences of something, the presence of the right-ordering of creation according to the plan of God. Christians must work not simply to stop conflict, but to cooperate with God in establishing the right-ordering of human relationships, setting the world aright where each of God's children has his or her share of the inheritance of the earth that God, the father of each, has willed for his child. There is no peace when a child is hungry. There is no peace when an old man is living without proper shelter. There is no peace when someone lacks the clothes needed to keep warm. There is no peace when a child lacks a future because there is no school in which he can learn. There is no peace when a person dies for lack of medication that could save her. There is no peace when persons lack basic human rights because of the colour of their skin or the religion they practices or that they are female rather than male. There is no peace when neither the unborn child, nor the sick and elderly can be guaranteed their life will be protected. There is no peace without the just ordering of the world according to the plan of God. The injustice that grips our world, the hopelessness of over a third of the human race who do not have the minimum gifts needed for survival, is the breeding ground of terrorism. Those who would have us believe that Islam is the seedbed of terrorism would have us make Islam the foe so that we would not look and see how the greed and selfishness of a small percentage of the world's inhabitants have cause poverty and suffering for many hundreds of millions. This poverty and suffering is the seedbed of terrorism, and not a few of those who are responsible for this injustice are Christians, indeed Catholics. This is why Pope John Paul spoke so often about the need to relieve the debt of poor nations so that they can begin to build the educational and medical infrastructures that can give their people hope. To be shod in the shoes of peace we must be working for the justice of the Kingdom of God, a world in which each of God's children has the hope of reaching the destiny for which God has created that child.

Our faith is our shield. Our faith is that which protects us from the attacks of our enemy which, Paul tells us, is no enemy of flesh and blood, but an enemy that attacks the spirit. God will fight the battle for us as he did so often for Israel of old, but as for Israel of old, we must fight it exactly as he tells us to fight it. We cannot divide our confidence–half in our own efforts and half of what God will do for us, half in our cunning, half in the divine plan. We must do it entirely his way. In other words, we must adhere to the Gospel of his Son, as counter-intuitive as it may seem to be in the given situation. The scripture warns us to "put not your strength in princes, in men in whom there is no salvation" (Psalm 146:3). The Gospel will prevail. It would be naïve to think that there will not be casualties in the fight, but our faith tells us to stay with the Gospel because the Gospel will be victorious in the end.

Paul tells us to put on the helmet of salvation. This is God's own headpiece; the one Isaiah says God wears in his battle when he takes up the cause of the afflicted in Isaiah 59. The helmet protects the head, as the shield, faith, protects the body. God has saved us, we are secure in this battle. But salvation is more than safety, more than "security." Salvation means, in its root, to be healthy, to be delivered from danger whether that danger be inflicted by another or proceeds from some physical ailment or flaw. We are restored to wholeness in salvation, indeed we are stronger than ever. This is not a gift we can attain, but only one which we can be given. Salvation, whether on the spiritual or physical plane, is a gift from God. There is only one who can give us salvation, Jesus Christ, because he alone can deliver us from sin. (cf Mt. (1:21)

We are to take up the Sword of the Spirit, that is the Word of God. We fight armed with the Word of God. Faith, our shield, is our defensive weapon. The Word of God, our Sword of the Spirit, is our offensive weapon. We aggressively wield the Word of God, that is to say we live the Word of God. We combat evil by taking God's Word and putting it into practice. This completes Paul's teaching on the Armour of God. When he wrote the *Pattern for Life* for the hermits on Mount Carmel, Albert took up this theme. He made it part of the hermits' life, and consequently part of the life and spirituality of each person who is committed to be a Carmelite, whether a Friar, a cloistered Nun, a Religious Sister, or a Lay Carmelite.

In giving the formula of life to guide the hermits in their spiritual battle, Albert made some modifications in the text of Paul's letter to the Ephesians, even as Paul had modified Isaiah and Wisdom to write about spiritual warfare. Some of Albert's modifications are not as drastic as they seem, but only interpreting Paul's original text as it would have been understood by most theologians in the Middle Ages. Other changes are more substantial, but they are not meant to replace Paul's exhortations, but rather to give the Carmelite a unique perspective of what might be expected of him in spiritual warfare, a perspective above and beyond, but not in place of, what is enjoined on all Christians.

The first change we notice is one of the more substantial changes. Whereas Paul instructs his listeners to gird their loins with the truth, Albert tells the hermits that their loins are to be girt with chastity. This does not excuse them from the Truth, obviously, an injunction placed on all believers, but demands of them an additional duty, a duty that Albert had somewhere to make explicit as the original hermits on Mount Carmel took only a vow of obedience and did not formally profess chastity. Only when Pope Innocent IV modified Albert's *Formula Vitae* 1247 and made the Carmelites canonically Religious, were the vows of poverty (renunciation of ownership) and chastity added to the Rule. Thus it was important that somewhere in the text Albert include this virtue which is so central to any form of Religious Life. Of course all Christians are called to chastity according to their state of life, but Albert was here calling the hermits to something above and beyond the common call. In the Middle Ages, an injunction to chastity was an injunction to celibacy. Although the lay hermits were not yet formally Religious who were required to vow celibacy, their commitment to the eremitical life required them to the practice of this particular type of chastity. If they did all else that the rule commanded, but did not live chastely, they would not have given any witness to the world of the power of the Gospel. Celibate chastity set these Christian hermits apart from the Muslims from whom they were trying to win the land for Christ. Although Islamic law required the Muslim to respect the honour of married women and unmarried Muslim virgins, male chastity was no virtue for the Muslim. Thus celibate chastity gave the Christian a particular weapon to use in this spiritual warfare, a weapon not accessible to his Muslim foe, but also a weapon little valued by his lay counterpart among the Christian warriors who were not necessarily known for their sexual temperance. This chastity was in fact a powerful weapon, for voluntary male chastity caused a respectful astonishment among Muslim warriors. Indeed their lives of sexual abstinence was one of the reasons that Christian monks were generally treated with respect in Muslim society and why male Religious could be used effectively as ambassadors to Islamic courts well past the Middle Ages into the seventeenth century. Precisely because it was so countercultural, it was a strong witness, a powerful weapon. To be effective it had to be honoured in reality and not merely a virtue that was talked about. Chastity today, celibate chastity for the Religious and unmarried Lay Carmelite, and chastity within the vocation of marriage for the married Carmelite, is still a powerful witness and counter-cultural value. Married people are not called to celibacy, but their witness of the sacredness of human sexuality which expresses the sacramental nature of the vocation of marriage, is much needed in the "post-Christian" west which has trivialized and de-sacralized the sexual relationship by separating it from marriage. Indeed, if we are ever to recover a sense of the sacred breaking into everyday existence and transforming this world into the Kingdom of God, it must begin with recovering the sacredness of the sexual by restoring it to its proper context of marriage. Strong and faithful sexual expression of marital love, the very heart of the sacrament of matrimony, is indeed a strong weapon in winning the world for Christ, every bit as strong as the celibate chastity of the Religious.

Albert next adds a weapon not mentioned by Paul when he writes "Your breast fortified by holy meditations." A literal translation from the Latin text is "holy thoughts" as the medieval understanding of meditation was somewhat different than ours. Systematic discursive meditation became popular in the *devotio moderna* of the fifteenth century, but these hermits were well used to holy thoughts rooted in the scriptures that had been read to them at Mass or in the Divine Office. They were used to hearing the Word of God and then thoughtfully considering the Word they had listened to as they went about the tasks of the day. These holy thoughts, reflections on the Word of God, were very much at the heart of the prayer life of these hermits. Earlier in the Rule Albert had instructed them that they should reflect on the Law of the Lord day and night. This meditation does not replace the breastplate of justice or holiness commanded by Paul, for Albert too tells the Carmelite to put on holiness as our breastplate, but fortifying our breast with holy meditation provides an added protection to us in this battle. It fact it is meditation, reflection on the Word of God, that endows us with the holiness, the righteousness, the justice that is our breastplate. Our immersion into the Word of God shows us the path of righteousness. Our righteousness is not simply some external behaviour, but is the fruit of our contemplation of God's Word that transforms us, by grace, into the person whom God has called us to be. Our meditation is not highly abstract and deeply pious flights of fancy, but our meditation is to show us how to be holy with our feet on the ground, how to make real and incarnate the love of God and of neighbour. Our meditation is directed to this one end–how we may love God and love our neighbour, because it is in this love of God and our neighbour that we fulfil the law of Christ. Once again, the righteousness, holiness, justice demanded of us is not mere piety, but the right ordering of relationships–the undivided love of God and the love of neighbour as ourselves. If we love God with an undivided heart and love our neighbour as ourselves, then we will share in this holiness which will protect us as a breastplate. So many hear the Gospel and strive for this ideal of fulfilling the two great commandments, but cannot ever make real progress because they cannot imagine what the commandments require in the concrete situation of life. But for us, meditation is precisely where the Word of God intersects with the realities of our lives.

For Albert, as for Paul, faith is our shield, the shield that extinguishes the flaming darts of the enemy, but Albert goes further. He says, in a very Pauline fashion, that there can be no pleasing God without faith. In fact, Albert finds this thought in chapter eleven of the Letter to the Hebrews which goes through the list of the patriarchs who pleased God by faith–Abel, Enoch, Noah, Abraham, Issac and Jacob. God protected them because they put their faith in him. And God will protect us too if we live by faith in God and in the One whom God has sent. As Paul makes so clear in his Epistles to the Romans and to the Galatians, we are set right with God by faith, we are justified by faith. Our relationship with God is a relationship based not on human efforts, but on our reception of God's grace of faith. And thus, the victory–which is beyond our winning, which only God can win–is won by faith. But can we walk clothed only in the armour of God? Is our faith sufficient that we trust God that his spiritual armaments are enough to win the battle against evil? Or will we falter and think that the armour of God needs the supplementary armour of human warfare? This is the nub of faith. This is the frightening demand of faith. We cannot put our trust in God and in princes. Faith demands it be in God alone. Faith demands that we confront the enemy of terrorism armed only with the weapons of God; that we not resort to responses outside the Gospel but that we trust that the Word of God is sufficient weapon for us to meet evil and overcome it. This is where the Christian is separated from the person who claims to be a disciple of Jesus but insists on covering his bets.

Medieval theology distinguished between three levels of faith, *credere Deum, credere Deo*, and *credere in Deum. Credere Deum* means to believe there is a God. Even the demons do this. *Credere Deo* means to believe in God. All religious people do this. For most Catholics this means that we accept true doctrine. We believe in the Trinity, in the divinity of Christ, the real presence of Christ in the Eucharist, and so forth. Sadly, for many, even those who consider themselves devout, that is all that faith means. But *credere in Deum*, to put your trust in God means to accept all that God has revealed, not merely as a matter of assent, but in practice. We must take God at his word. Or, as Jesus says, "Blessed are those who hear the Word of God and observe it. (Luke 11:28)." *Credere in Deum* requires of us that we take God at his Word and that we shape our lives accordingly.

Methodist theologian Stanley Hauerwas tells a wonderful story about the difference between *credere Deo* and *credere in Deum*.

> Clarence Jordan was the founder of the Koinonia Farm near Americus Georgia. It was set up to be an interracial community before anyone knew what civil rights were all about. Jordan himself was a pacifist as well as an integrationist and thus was not a popular figure in Georgia, even though he came from a prominent family.
>
> The Koinonia Farm, by its very nature, was controversial and, of course, it was in trouble. McClendon reports that in the early fifties Clarence approached his brother Robert Jordan (later a state senator and justice of the Georgia Supreme Court) to ask him to legally represent the Koinonia Farm. Robert responded to Clarence's request:
>
> "Clarence, I can't do that. You know my political aspirations. Why if I represented you, I might lose my job, my house, everything I've got."

"We might lose everything too, Bob."
"It's different for you."
"Why is it different? I remember, it seems to me, that you and I joined the church the same Sunday, as boys. I expect when we came forward the preacher asked me about the same question he did you. He asked me, 'Do you accept Jesus as your Lord and Saviour.' And I said, 'yes.' What did you say?"
"I follow Jesus, Clarence, up to a point."
"Could that point by any chance be–the cross?"
"That's right. I follow him to the cross, but not on the cross. I'm not getting myself crucified."
"Then I don't believe you're a disciple. You're an admirer of Jesus, but not a disciple of his.[17]

These are harsh words from brother to brother, but they get to the heart of the dilemma. Are we willing to take Jesus at his word? Hauerwas goes on to write a reflection about the two disciples on the way to Emmaus, a reflection that illustrates how we disarm the teachings of Jesus by considering him an inspiring idealist rather than Lord and Saviour.

That we find these two on the way to Emmaus, walking away from Jerusalem, gives us some basis for thinking that they were admirers, not unlike Robert Jordan. They clearly understood that what had been taking place in Jerusalem around this man Jesus con-

---

[17] Stanley Hauerwas, "The Insufficiency of Scripture," *Unleashing the Scripture,: Freeing the Bible from Captivity to America,* Nashville: Abingdon Press, 1993. pp. 50-51.

cerned very serious matters indeed. In fact, they were continuing to discuss it in an effort to understand what had taken place. Maybe they were not admirers. Perhaps they were intellectuals or even theologians. One can almost hear them say, "That was really an interesting set of suggestions Jesus had to make about the kingdom. Damned insightful, though a bit overstated I must say. Though he is quite provocative, he really lacks the characteristics of a carefully trained mind"[18]

In the same way many people today say that we have to adapt the words of Jesus to modern realities. "Insightful, but not practical, this Jesus," many think to themselves. "All this stuff about loving your enemies and praying for your persecutors, not returning evil for evil…it sounds fine when you read it in church, but what kind of a world would we have if people actually took Jesus at his word?" What kind of a world indeed! We must ask ourselves what kind of faith we have. Is it only the faith that tells us Jesus is truly present in the Eucharist, or is it the sort of faith that shapes the way we live day by day, the way we vote, the television we watch, the schools to which we send our children, the friends with whom we socialize, the values for which we speak up. Are we disciples, or are we admirers? To be a soldier winning the world for Christ with the armour of God, we must be disciples.

Albert, like Paul, has us don the helmet of salvation, but he elaborates on this as well. We think of

---

[18] Stanley Hauerwas, "The Insufficiency of Scripture," pp. 51-52.

salvation only in terms of eternal salvation, but that is not what the word means. The Latin term used in the Rule, *salus*, while it does theologically mean salvation, also is the ordinary word used in every day language for safety. It also can be used for health. Salvation, that is our victory in this cosmic battle, is won only by God for us. But neither Albert nor Paul limit the meaning to the idea of eternal salvation. Not only is our only salvation in Christ, our only safety in the temporal realm of things is in Christ. The only path to peace in the temporal order of things is the Gospel of Christ. If we want safety for ourselves and for our children, we must live the Gospel ourselves and hope that this confidence in Christ will spread. Neither in the eternal nor the temporal order is there salvation other than that which is offered us in Christ. Christ delivers us, we do not save ourselves. Salvation is always a gift given, never a reward earned. The Muslim warriors who faced the crusaders believed that if they died in battle, their sins were forgiven and they went straight to paradise. This same belief has been the encouraging myth that has sent so many contemporary suicide bombers on their way to wreak terror and havoc. We know, of course, that acts of violence do not win salvation, but we must remember that our salvation cannot be won, in either a temporal or an eternal sense, by violence. Violence begets violence. Until we break the chain of violence, there will be no salvation and their will be no safety.

Finally, we are to arm ourselves with the Sword of the Spirit, the Word of God, even as Paul has enjoined us. But again Albert adds his little commentary. This Word of God must abound on our mouths and in our hearts. We must be immersed into the Word of God. The Word of God is our plan for battle. We meet the foe armed with the Word of God. This is a powerful Word, a Word that reverses human insight and wisdom and demands of us the unthinkable. Yet it is not something esoteric or mystical. It is something right at hand for us. When Albert says that the Word of God must dwell in our minds and in our hearts he is referring to Deuteronomy 30:14 where the scripture says that the law which God imposes on the people is not something mysterious or remote. It is not something up in the sky or far across the sea. It is already in our possession. We Christians who have received the Gospel of Christ know this. We already have the saving Word, we have the path to peace. We have the means of safety. It is the Gospel of Christ and it is very real, very concrete. We must love our enemies and pray for our persecutors. We must feed our enemy when he is hungry and care for him while he is sick. We must surrender not only what he takes from us, but indeed surrender over to him anything that he needs. In other words, we must meet his violence with the peace that only Christ can give us.

This spiritual warfare found in Paul and expanded for us Carmelites in Albert has the potential for radically shifting the ground of the battle from a war between nations and cultures and religions to the battle that it truly is, the battle between humanity and its great foe who has always wanted to see humankind divided against itself in hopes of bringing down the destiny of humankind, the Kingdom of God. For Christians to meet those who call themselves our enemy with offers of reconciliation, of peace, of cooperation in building a world in which each person, regardless of race or nationality or religion, can have a future shifts the ground of the battle dramatically. To take the most passionately expressed ideal of Pope John Paul, the ideal that has defined every teaching of his papacy, Solidarity, and apply it as a projected offer for the future–that is to propose that instead of working towards opposing ends we begin working for a common future–offers an alternative to the escalating culture of death that is dragging our world into a hell of conflict, war, and violence.. The objection will surely be made that "they," (meaning the Islamic extremists) are interested only in the triumph and domination of Islam over the (post) Christian West. But let us be honest, the defeat and subjection of Islam has been the goal of the voices of the "Christian Right" that have been rattling swords other than the Sword of the Spirit, that is the Word of God, ever since the downfall of the last enemy, Communism. Islam has been excoriated by self-styled evangelicals who have blasphemed the Name of Jesus by proposing that their crusades are in his Name. The fact of the matter is that true disciples of Christ, those who truly hear his Word and put it into practice, look for a world in which no person is defeated, but in which Christ is revealed as Messiah by the effective implementation of his Gospel. Once again, we Christians know that there are things for which we must be willing to die, but true disciples of Jesus know, despite a bloody and guilty history of Crusades and Inquisitions, that there is nothing for which we can kill.[19] Any earthly victory is only temporary. Every time we pray the Lord's Prayer, we ask God to finally put the plan Christ has revealed, the Kingdom of God, into practice in the earthly order of things as he has already in the heavenly order. But this kingdom cannot be a reality until we submit to it in obedience to the teachings of Christ. Thus the disciple of Jesus must not resort to violence in winning the world for Christ. Nothing will retard the coming of the Kingdom more than turning to violence, not because violence is in some way worse than sin, but because violence against human life is the worst of sins. Thus the Christian is bound to search for means of dialogue with Islam, not conflict. Shortly after September 11th, Pope John Paul II said,

"I wish to reaffirm the Catholic Church's respect for Islam, for authentic Islam: The Islam that prays, that is concerned for those in need. ...Hatred, fanaticism and terrorism profane the name of God and disfigure the true image of man,"

We Christians must also take these words of John Paul to heart. Christians must not use hatred, fanaticism, and violence to profane the name of God and disfigure the true image of humankind.

Benedict XVI seemed to veer from his predecessor's respect for authentic Islam when, giving a lecture at the

---

[19] While this is my phrasing, it is not my insight but is taken from Stanley Hauerwas and William H. Willimon, *Resident Aliens: Life in the Christian Colony*, Nashville:Abingdon, 1989, p. 148

University of Regensburg on September 12, 2006, he quoted Byzantine Emperor Manuel II Paleologus who, in a 1391 dialogue with an unnamed Persian scholar, had said:

"Show me just what Mohammed brought that was new, and there you will find things only evil and inhuman, such as his command to spread by the sword the faith he preached."

However when one reads the pertinent passages of the Pope's speech at the University of Regensburg, one sees the context of this quote was not to accuse Islam of a history of violence, but rather to open the door to discuss the relationship between reason (as opposed to force) and religious conviction. In the ensuing controversy over the address, Benedict made it very clear that he by no means endorsed the views of the Emperor, much less did he make them his own. The history of Islam has been tarnished by violence, but no more so than the history of Christianity. Islamic extremists who advocate violence bring disgrace on Islam and its Prophet, even as Christians who advocate repaying violence for violence betray their Lord whose Gospel makes no such allowance.

The Christian is caught in a conflict of loyalties when his nation embarks on a program of violence in the name of seeking security and this conflict should give us pause for serious reflection. How each of us resolves the tension is a matter for our own conscience, but resolve it we must. We cannot stand with a foot in both camps. No man can serve two masters. The choice is set before us, whom shall we serve? Yet this

A Final Reflection

dilemma is not easy to resolve. Our true citizenship, Paul tells us, is in heaven (Philippians 3:20) But this does not absolve us from our duties as citizens of an earthly realm. We must bring our faith to bear on the decisions we make for political leadership, even as we must bring our faith to bear on every decision we make. We cannot take responsibility for the leaders of the world and the decisions that they make. It is not their plan to win the world for Christ in any event. Their interest is in winning the world for themselves and for the interests of the nations they lead. Their wars are not fought in the name of Christ and it attacks the integrity of the Gospel when they claim that they are using their tanks and missiles for a Christian cause, or in the name of God. Whatever the course which go our various nations, as Christians we must reject any options in life that are not compatible with the Gospel of Christ. We ourselves cannot fight this battle with evil, in whatever form it takes, with any arms other than those given us by God. We must trust that God has revealed in Christ a plan for humankind to find its destiny in God and we must either embrace that plan or have the integrity to realize that despite our sentimental attachment to Christian traditions we are no longer Christian. We may be admirers of Christ, but we have chosen not to be his disciples. And as Carmelites, as heirs of those hermits on Mount Carmel who faced the foe in their mountain valley with the weapons of the Gospel, we must take the responsibility to fight to win the world for Christ but using his arms. We are not to abstain from the fight, we are not pacifists, but we must take up the weapons allowed us and trust that the assurances that God has given that his victory will be won with these arms is sufficient promise for us. This may sound naïve or idealistic, but we need to recall the words of Chesterton: "The Christian ideal has not been tried and found wanting, it has been found difficult and left untried." Our world is on a desperate course of violence as the post-Christian west and the Islamic world collide. The battle can only be won by God. The Church gives us a sobering reflection in the Office of readings.

"Those who have been considered worthy to go forth as the sons of God and to be born again of the Holy Spirit, from on high, and who hold within them the Christ who renews them and fills them with light, are directed by the Spirit in varied and different ways and in their repose they are led invisibly in their hearts by grace.... At one time they are like a brave man who puts on the king's full armour and goes down into battle, he fights bravely against the enemy and defeats them. In like manner, the spiritual man takes up the heavenly armour of the Spirit and marches against the enemy and engaging in battles tramples the foes beneath his feet."[20]

It is for us to choose, to be disciples or to be admirers, to be found worthy to go forth as the children of God, born again in the Holy Spirit, or to be people of this world who put their confidence in the earthly solu-

---

[20] Office of Readings, Friday, fourth week in ordinary time, an unnamed "spiritual author of the fourth century."

tion to problems of eternal significance. To take possession of the world for Christ, we must let Christ take possession of us. The issue is transformation–we must be transformed into Christ. This is, of course, precisely what all Christian spirituality is about. I have been crucified with Christ, it is no longer I who live, it is Christ Jesus who lives in me. If it is Christ Jesus who lives in us, we must fight the battle against evil as he fought it–with compassion for our enemies, mercy for those who have sinned against us, and the weight of the cross pressing on us, not inflicted on others.

As Carmelites we have a particular vocation to win the world for Christ. We join out fellow citizens in the conflict, but we are called by our Carmelite vocation fight the battle with different weapons. We have come to see with the eyes of faith that the methods of this world will not suffice to bring the peace that only Christ can bestow. It is a crucial vocation, a prophetic vocation, to stand faithful to the Word of God and trusting in the Word of God. But we believe that Christ indeed is the only Saviour and that any hope for peace, true peace, can be found only in his Word. Our contemplative vocation transforms us to men and women of compassionate peace and we are confident that the Gospel has this power to transform each and every person in Christ Jesus. We are therefore ardently missionaries of the Gospel, preaching by example rather than words. We have seen that war only begets war, violence only begets violence, and that the chain of this mass insanity must be broken. We have also seen that compassion begets compassion, mercy generates mercy, forgiveness teaches forgiveness. We know that Christ offers an alternative to the madness and the Gospel is the way to peace, true peace–not merely the cessation of war, always a temporary cessation–but the establishment of the bonds of Christian fraternity which will bring solidarity, justice, healing, and the peace which only Christ can give. But this requires of us a commitment to take up the armour of God with all the passion of true warriors. We must admit to no compromise. We must defend ourselves with true integrity, hard-rock and uncompromising fidelity to what we profess. We must be men and women of chastity according to our particular vocation. This means far more than avoiding personal sin. In a world in which people are routinely exploited, whether for personal pleasure or for corporate gain, we must see the sacredness of each human life. We must refuse to participate in the culture of exploitation in our choices of entertainment. We must use the power of our purse, no matter how seemingly insignificant, to resist the commercialism that exploits people in advertising, in unjust labour practices, in contributing to the culture of exploitation. We must be sure that we ourselves, neither directly nor indirectly, contribute to the exploitation of others for cheap labour. This requires that we be informed and knowledgeable about issues such as globalization and the economy. If this seems "too worldly" we need to remember Jesus' admonition that while we are to be as innocent as doves, we must be as wise as serpents. We cannot afford to be ill-informed. There is nothing holy or spiritual about being ignorant accomplices of evil. This is war, we must take it seriously.

We must fortify ourselves with holy mediations. We must be faithful to mental prayer. We must give ourselves over at every available moment to pondering the Word of God and applying it to the concrete reality of our lives. These holy thoughts will protect us. They will open to us the concrete ways in which our good will becomes actual love for God and love for our neighbour. Carmelites have a passion to reflect on the Word of God. And once fortified with the Word of God we can put on the breastplate of Justice. Justice will fit us well once we have immersed ourselves in the Word of God. Justice is the application of that Word to the concrete reality of our lives. We will be people who understand through meditation and act in righteousness.

Faith will be our shield. We can trust God, standing firm and faithful in his Word, in the most perilous moments. When others give in and make compromising choices, we can stand firm. When those around us yield to the temptations of revenge, of anger, of a thirst for violence, we can stand firm in our faith in Christ and his word. With our fellow citizens, we will give Caesar his due, but we will not compromise our faithfulness to Christ and to his Gospel in doing so. We will remember that we stand faithful to a higher authority and we will not compromise that loyalty. We will not buy the lies that Caesar or his minions use to try to wean us from our commitment to the Gospel of Peace. Faith will be our shield and protect us from the darts of the Evil One. We will not be seduced into violence with promises that it can bring us "peace." Only Christ and his Gospel can bring peace.

We will put on the helmet of salvation which is Christ himself. We will put on Christ. Through prayer and meditation we will seek to conform ourselves to

Christ, to mould our wills to his so that we "fit him a like a glove." The key is this transformation into Christ. When it is no longer we who live, but Christ Jesus who lives in us, the battle is won. When the whole world becomes conformed to Christ then there can be peace. We may think this is an impossibility, but would Christ have sent us on an impossible mission? It is a tremendous task, of course, a mission of overwhelming scope, but it begins with you and me. It begins with our conversion. We must simply do our part and allow God to do the rest.

And finally, we fight with only one weapon, the weapon allowed us by God, the Sword of the Spirit, that is the Word of God. We must know that Word. We must immerse ourselves in that Word. We must allow that Word to be the sole guide for our lives. Our faith is in that Word. This is not simply some word on a page, even the page of a holy book. This is a living Word, a Word that has become incarnate in Jesus Christ. Is Christ enough for us? We cannot wield this Sword of the Spirit if anything else is in our hands. We must let go of all that is not Christ, not only the sinful, but even the good that is not him. We must cling only to Christ. We see the difference that a person for whom Christ is their all can make–we see a Francis of Assisi, for example–and we see the power for change that the Word can be in our world. People come to Christ because of a Francis, or a Mother Theresa. We too must have the courage to belong totally to Christ and allow him to be our only treasure, for when we possess Christ, and are possessed by him, we find that we meet all the world in Christ. Every face

A Final Reflection

we see becomes Christ for us. Every person becomes the object of our love. It is only when more and more of us Christians come to this transformation that the tide of the battle will finally turn and love can overcome violence. This is not a vocation for Religious alone, it is a vocation for all would follow Jesus Christ. We can win the world for Christ. Ultimately it is a matter of grace, but the grace has been given. It was given on the day of our baptism, and it was renewed on the day we entered Carmel. It now requires only that we yield to it. So put on the armour of God so that you can stand firm on the evil day and, having done everything, hold firm your ground.

The translations of the Rule are, for the most part, from

Constitutions of the Order of the Brothers of the Blessed Virgin Mary of Mount Carmel. *Approved by the General Chapter celebrated in September, 1995 and published by the order of the Most Reverend Father Joseph Chalmers, Prior General.*

Chapters have been renumbered since the Rule was published in 1995. The Chapter numbers used above are the result of a joint meeting of the General Councils of the Carmelites and the Discalced Carmelites in January, 1999.

Innocentian additions are given in italics.

(Translation by Fr. Bede Edwards, originally published in The Rule of Saint Albert, ed. Hugh Clarke & Bede Edwards, Aylesford and Kensington, 1973)

Finito di stampare
nel mese di Giugno 2007
dalla tipografia Abilgraph srl